Money

Money

HOW TO MAKE IT,
SPEND IT,
AND
KEEP LOTS OF IT

TODD TEMPLE

FOREWORD BY MARY HUNT
FOUNDER AND PUBLISHER OF *CHEAPSKATE MONTHLY*

BROADMAN
& HOLMAN
PUBLISHERS

Nashville, Tennessee

© 1998
by Todd Temple
Printed in the United States of America

0-8054-0168-7

Published by Broadman & Holman Publishers, Nashville, Tennessee
Acquisitions and Development Editor: Janis Whipple
Page Design: Anderson Thomas Design
Page Compositor: PerfecType, Nashville, Tennessee

Dewey Decimal Classification: 332.024
Subject Heading: TEENAGERS—UNITED STATES—FINANCE, PERSONAL
Library of Congress Card Catalog Number: 97-51244

Published in association with the literary agency of Alive Communications, Inc.,
1465 Kelly Johnson Blvd., Suite 320, Colorado Springs, Colorado 80920

Unless otherwise stated all Scripture citation is from the NIV, the Holy Bible, New
International Version, copyright © 1973, 1978, 1984 by International Bible Society

Library of Congress Cataloging-in-Publication Data
Temple, Todd, 1958-
Money : how to make it, spend it, and keep lots of it / Todd Temple
p. cm.
ISBN 0-8054-0168-7 (tp)
1. Teenagers—United States—Finance, Personal. 2. Finance, Personal.
I. Title.
HG179.T412   1997
332.024—dc21

97-51244
CIP

1 2 3 4 5 02 01 00 99 98

Dedication

To Stephanie, Michael, Kathleen,
Natalie, Thomas, Josh, and Kaitlin

Acknowledgments

As you'll soon see, this book has lots of information in it—far more than I could ever store inside my brain. Fortunately, I had more than one brain to work with: If not for the ideas, experiences, and knowledge stored in the sharp brains of my friends in the business and financial worlds, this would be a much thinner book. Among these wise folk, I would especially like to thank Randy O'Connell for his friendship and frequent financial guidance both personal and professional, and Dr. Mike Watson for his assistance in the chapter on buying a car—his expertise in this field comes from a habit nearly as old as our three-decade friendship.

I would also like to thank Navid Mahooti for his research, Carolyn Poirier for her editorial assistance and encouragement throughout the project, and my agent Greg Johnson at Alive Communications and Janis Whipple at Broadman & Holman for bringing this project to life.

Table of Contents

Part Three
Giving Money

Part Four
Saving Money

Part Five
Spending Money

Foreword

How much money have you received from the day you were born until right now? You haven't a clue? Well, take a guess. OK, now check this out: By the time the average kid in this country turns twenty, he or she will have received more than $33,000 in income and gifts of money. And that's not typo. Where did all your money go, you ask? That's exactly what I was going to ask you.

Just thinking about 33 G's slipping through your fingers should make you wince with pain. I hope it does, because that means you're ready to read this book. I'm telling you, Todd Temple is fabulous and he's going to teach you how to become the kind of steward God can trust to take care of money.

Let me tell you something about myself. I have the attention span of a gnat and I read about 4.3 words per minute. A book has to be pretty terrific to keep me turning the pages. Now get this: I read *Money: How to Make It, Spend It, and Keep Lots of It* straight through, over to cover, beginning to end. Rolling on the floor with laughter didn't make it any easier, either. But I did it, I loved it, and I know you will too.

When I was a teen I had some pretty whacky ideas about money. I believed money was power, pleasure, freedom, happiness, security, and choices. And I had to go through some pretty rotten times to learn my belief was completely false—a big, fat zero. *Money: How to Make It, Spend It, and Keep Lots of It* will teach you it's not money, but what you do with your money—the way you behave with it—that can produce power, pleasure, freedom, happiness, security, and choices. Money on its own is not important, but options are. And money bestows options.

One last thing. When you finish this book, send Todd a letter and tell him what you think about it. It'll make his day. Authors are like that.

Mary Hunt
Co-founder and Publisher of *Cheapskate Monthly*
Author of *Tiptionary* and
The Financially Confidant Woman

Part One

Basic Money Stuff You Gotta Know

This book is going to tell you just about everything you need to know about money right now, such as how to:

Make money (that's in Part 2)

Give money (that's Part 3)

Save money (that's Part 4)

Spend money (and that's Part 5)

But before we explore all the cool things you can do with money, we need to talk about money itself: who's got it, who wants it, and how to keep track of it all. This is important stuff—stuff you gotta know. That's what this first part is about.

So what are you waiting for? Let's get started!

Chapter 1
Take Back Your Wallet

When I was three years old, I had my front teeth bashed in. I didn't do it on purpose—I just happened to be smiling at a large rock when it decided to fall. I'll save you from the gory, chard-spitting details and jump to the dentist's chair; the dentist had to cover the stubby remains of my front teeth with two giant silver caps.

Years later, when my adult teeth grew in, the silver-capped teeth fell out. By then, I was well acquainted with the tooth fairy's redemption plan—when you hide a tooth under your pillow at night, you'll wake up to find money in its place. Back when I was a kid, a regular old tooth was worth a quarter. (Maybe her rates have gone up by now . . . I don't know.) So I figured that a *silver* tooth had to be worth much more than a quarter. Sure enough, the morning after I placed the first, shiny, silver tooth under my pillow, I awoke to find that the tooth fairy had left an even shinier silver *dollar*. The same thing

happened with the other silver tooth a few days later. Now I had two silver dollars! I was rich—and the envy of every kid I knew.

This story has a sad ending. Months after the fairy's visits I discovered the awful truth—there *was* no tooth fairy. She was a myth. Apparently, my dad had delivered the dental dollars. I was so distraught, I went out and spent the silver coins. On Pez, I think.

I hope that your own discovery of the tooth fairy's nonexistence wasn't so traumatic. (And if that revelation didn't come until just this moment, I'm sorry to spoil the fun.) But I've got news for you—the tooth fairy is not the only money myth out there. Read on.

MONEY MYTHS

Chances are, you're clinging to quite a few financial fictions. But unlike the nocturnal tooth exchange, the other money myths don't make you richer. They make you poorer.

Here's the biggest money myth among teenagers: *Money stuff doesn't matter, till you're older.* Most teenagers figure that between an allowance, odd jobs, minimum-wage paychecks, and an occasional birthday check there's not enough money to worry about. What good are budgets when there's so little cash to manage?

A lot of adults in this world are delighted to know that you think that way. Because as long as you do, you'll

Michael Jordan makes over $20 million a year from Nike endorsements alone.

keep giving them your money. *Your ignorance about money is making people rich.* I'll show you.

The average American teenager spends over $2,400 a year. Multiply that average by your 29 million teenage peers, and you've got $70 billion. And that's just the money spent by teenagers themselves. Your parents spend another large stack on you for clothes, gifts, and groceries. You have a strong influence on how they spend this money for you, which comes to $40 billion.

Now add these two giant stacks of cash: *$110 billion!* In other words, American teenagers are responsible for spending $110 billion *each year,* and that number is growing. Now these figures may not mean that much to you, but to marketers they mean *everything.*

Marketers are the people and companies that make and sell stuff: fast food, soft drinks, candy, snacks, clothing, shoes, CDs, software, computers, cosmetics, deodorant, games, sports equipment, and anything else you buy with your cash. They see that glorious $110 billion figure, and they want their share. Marketers enlist armies of researchers, recruit celebrity athletes, spend billions on advertising, and do everything else in their power to get *your* money into *their* pockets.

Let's look at how the numbers work. Let's say McDonald's wants a share of your $110 billion. What if they could get every teenager in America to spend just two bucks each week at their restaurants? That's $104 out of your pocket each year. No big deal . . . until you remember that there are 28 million other teenage mouths

to feed. In that case, they'd bring in nearly $3 billion!

What if every teenager bought a single pair of "cheap" $50 Nike shoes each year? The company would bring in $1.4 billion. It's no wonder they can spend millions on big-time athletes to spruce up their commercials.

Your tiny stack of cash, added with every other teenager's little money pile, adds up to a lot of money. The marketers want their share of that money, and they'll do just about anything to get it. I'm not ripping on McDonald's or Nike or any other company out there selling you stuff. I'm just saying that they're *experts* at selling to teenagers. So unless you figure out how to manage your money, you will lose the money game now and keep on losing the rest of your life.

> *You need to be as good at making and keeping your money as the marketers are at taking it.*

That's what this book is all about. How to take the control of your money out of the hands of the marketers and put it back where it belongs—with you. We'll explode some of the myths about money that have been passed down to you by those who seek to profit from your ignorance. I'm going to tell you things that the marketers *don't* want you to know. I'll show you their tricks and schemes . . . and how to outsmart them.

Warning: I'm going to say things that will make some people mad. Maybe even you. But remember that

"The problem with money is that it makes you do things you don't want to do." —Wall Street, the movie

there are tens of thousands of marketers eager to grab your cash. They have huge advertising budgets to convince you that you should give your cash to them. They stand to make billions on your mythical money beliefs. As for me, I've just got this little book to tell you the other side of the story. That means I'll have to shout pretty loud sometimes to get you to see the truth.

Here's the good news—you *can* win at the money game. You can make, save, and spend your money wisely. It doesn't matter if you're rich or poor, if you have $10,000 in savings or $10 in a piggy bank. The money tricks you'll learn here will help you get the most out of your money and do really great things with whatever you've got.

So let's get started. Jump to the next chapter. We're about to explode another money myth!

Chapter 2

Now Give It to Someone Else

In the first chapter, I kept talking about "your money." I used that term because I didn't want to scare you with all the facts right away. Now that we're friends, I feel comfortable telling you the whole truth. *It's not your money.*

It's God's money. I'm not saying that because I'm a Christian, or because this book was printed by a Christian publisher, or because maybe you bought it at a Christian bookstore. I'm saying it because it's true. Check it out for yourself:

> *For every animal of the forest is mine,*
> *and the cattle on a thousand hills.*
> *If I were hungry I would not tell you,*
> *for the world is mine, and all that is in it.*
> —Psalm 50:10, 12

Did you catch that last line? "For the world is mine, and all that is in it." God is the creator of the universe, the ultimate owner of everything in it. That includes you and your money.

The cool thing is, God has appointed you as "steward"—the official *manager* of the money he's entrusted to you. That's a big job. Over the course of your lifetime, you could be managing millions of his dollars. As you can expect, God has some strong opinions about what to do—and what not to do—with *his* money.

Actually, that's what makes money management fun. You're not just grappling with facts and figures and grimy stacks of coins and cash. You're an *asset* manager for the richest, most wonderful Boss in the universe. When you're a wise manager, you're in for some great benefits: a sense of accomplishment, the thrill of using money to help people in need, the opportunity to change the world for the better, and more time to spend with people you care about. And sometimes, you can buy cool stuff with some of his money.

Later in the book we'll talk about specific ways to give back God's money. For now, let's just leave it at this: Throughout the rest of the book, when we talk about "your money," you'll know who's money we're really talking about.

Chapter 3

Bonehead-Easy Guide to Money Management

Most people see the term *money management* and either fall asleep or break out in a sweat. The term sounds like something you do with a big computer and stacks of paper, receipts, ledgers, checkbooks, and a big, fat calculator. That's no fun. But it doesn't have to be that way.

In fact, money management can be bonehead easy and even kind of fun. I'll show you right now. Grab four envelopes and label them like this:

The next step is nearly as easy. Get four pieces of notebook paper. Put a title on the top of each, just like the labels on your envelopes: INCOME, GIVE, SAVE, SPEND.

The next trick is to put some lines on each of the pages, and give each column a heading: DATE, TRANSACTION, AMOUNT, BALANCE. When you're done, the columns on each page should look like this:

DATE	TRANSACTION	AMOUNT	BALANCE

Each of these pages is called a *ledger*. If you look in a checkbook, you'll find something that looks a lot like it, called a *register*. Basically, they're the same thing. Whatever you call it, you can use this format to keep track of money.

Now that you've got the envelopes and ledgers ready, it's time to use them. It's really very simple. When you earn money, you stick it in the INCOME envelope and write down the amount of the *deposit* on the income ledger.

Income goes in the INCOME envelope and gets recorded as a deposit in the ledger.

Of course the money doesn't do much good just sitting there in the envelope—you've got to move it around to put your money to work. Time to make some withdrawals. With your income you can do one of three things: You can *give* it, *save* it, or *spend* it. Let's say you've just earned 50 bucks and you want to give away 10% to your church. Go to your INCOME envelope, take out $5, and write down the amount of the *withdrawal* on the INCOME ledger. Then *deposit* the money in the GIVE envelope and record the transaction in the GIVE ledger. Here's what your ledgers will look like:

INCOME

DATE	TRANSACTION	AMOUNT	BALANCE
3/12	deposit	50.00	50.00
3/12	withdrawal	5.00	45.00

GIVE

DATE	TRANSACTION	AMOUNT	BALANCE
3/12	deposit	5.00	5.00
			5.00

In 1997, NBA star Grant Hill signed an $80 million endorsement contract with Fila.

You'll notice that I used two lines, or rows, for the GIVE ledger transaction. You can use just one line per entry (like I did on the INCOME ledger transactions) if you want to, but with two lines, you can easily add or subtract each new transaction from your *previous balance.*

Let's say that you also want to put 20% of your income (that $50) into savings. Withdraw $10 from your INCOME envelope, deposit it in the SAVE envelope, and record the two transactions on the appropriate ledgers.

Now you've got $35 left in your INCOME envelope. Withdraw it and make a deposit in your SPEND envelope. Now the entire $50 has been distributed among the three big *accounts,* and the INCOME envelope is empty.

There's just one more step. When you take money out of the GIVE envelope to give to your church or make some other kind of donation, be sure to write the transaction as a *withdrawal* to that account. Same thing with the SAVE envelope—when you're ready to make a deposit into your bank savings account, *withdraw* the money from the SAVE envelope and record it on the ledger. And if you take money out of the SPEND envelope, be sure to record the *withdrawal* on your SPEND ledger.

That's all there is to this system. First deposit all your money into the INCOME envelope, then distribute it to the other envelopes. I told you it was easy.

YOUR BUDGET

Of course, this system only works if you have a *budget*—a *plan* for distributing your money among your *priorities*. In the above example, I used a simple budget based on three priorities:

> *priority #1: GIVE 10% of my income.*
> *priority #2: SAVE 20% of my income.*
> *priority #3: SPEND what's left.*

Weekly Budget	
Income	+ $50
Giving (10%)	– $ 5
Saving (20%)	– $10
Spending	= $35

You can learn a lot about a person's priorities in life simply by looking at his or her budget. If the above budget were yours, I'd know three important things about you just by looking at your budget. First, you believe that God is the true owner of your money, and you acknowledge that fact by *giving* a chunk of it straight back to him. Second, you have big plans for your future, because you're *saving* money to fund those plans. And third, you're a real live human who *spends* money on other stuff.

Of course, if you have no budget at all, it's hard for others to tell what your priorities are. What's worse, without a budget *you* may not be able to recognize your priorities either.

A budget declares your priorities and *gives you a plan for carrying them out.*

The cool thing about the budget on page 13 is that it works on *percentages.* No matter how much money you make (or how little), you're committed to giving away a portion, saving another portion, and spending only what's left. One problem: What if your spending *habit* is bigger than your spending *budget*? Let's say that you typically spend $50 a week on food, transportation, fun stuff, whatever. If your *income* is just $50 a week, you'll bust your budget. That leaves you with three choices:

1. *Increase your income.*
2. *Decrease your spending.*
3. *Rearrange your priorities.*

Guess what? Most people choose option number 3. Actually, they don't really *choose* it—it chooses them. When they don't have enough spending money, they steal the cash out of their saving or giving accounts, which says, "Spending is more important."

When you make and keep a budget, *you* take control of your money. *You* decide how it's used. *You* get to choose your priorities. *You* determine how much money you need to earn and how much you can spend. Your world is filled with parents, teachers, and other adults who make the rules about how you should live. With a budget, *you* make the rules about your money. If you follow your rules, you'll have more freedom to do what's most important to you.

ACTION PLAN

Does that kind of independence sound good to you? Then act on it. Here's the plan:

1. **Make a budget.** Take a piece of paper and write down your financial priorities. Do you want to give? How much? Do you want to save money for something big in your future? How much? Based on your average weekly income, can you afford to live on what's left? If not, review the three choices above.

2. **Keep your budget.** Prepare the four envelopes and four ledgers I just showed you. Now, with your very next chunk of income, deposit it in your INCOME account, then distribute it among the GIVE, SAVE, and SPEND accounts. Don't borrow money from one account to use for something else: Spend only what you've budgeted, and deliver the other cash to its proper destinations. Now go through this same routine with every new bit of income.

It's really that simple! In a few weeks' time, this money management system will become a habit. Your giving will increase, your savings will grow, and you'll learn how to be smart with your spending. Then you can buy what's important and save the rest for bigger things ahead.

Bread, clams, dough, sugar, lettuce, and gravy are all names used for money.

15

Chapter 4

Big-Time Budgets and Accounting

Believe it or not, the money management system I just taught you is the same one used by smart millionaires, giant corporations, and financial gurus everywhere. Of course, they make a few modifications to the plan to handle larger budgets and longer priority lists. But the basic system is the same:

> *Make a budget based on your priorities. Keep a budget using separate accounts.*

You've probably already guessed that most wise money managers don't use envelopes to stow all their cash. When you start to make great piles of income, you can't really hide the cash in envelopes stuffed under your mattress (the lumps would make sleeping too difficult).

So instead of using a few little envelopes, they use one giant "envelope" called a *checking account.* You can do the same thing right now to track your own money.

Here's how it works: Instead of sticking your earnings in the INCOME envelope, you deposit all your income into your checking account. Your *check register* acts as your INCOME ledger. (The register is that little booklet in the back of a checkbook. It looks a lot like those ledgers I showed you in the last chapter, and it works the same way.) Let's use the amounts from the previous chapter to show you what happens.

GIVE ACCOUNT

First, deposit your $50 income into the checking account and write the deposit in your check register. Now go to your GIVE ledger and write down a deposit for $5. Here's the cool part. You don't actually have to put the $5 in the GIVE envelope. Just leave it in the checking account for now, but write down the deposit on the GIVE ledger, *just as if it were in a separate envelope.*

When it comes time to give that money to your church, you simply write a $5 check, record the withdrawal in your check register *and* your GIVE ledger. Yep, both places. At first this sounds a bit confusing, so let me give you a good analogy.

Let's say you and your friends decide to go swimming at the beach, pool, lake, or duck pond (take your pick). Each of you brings money for lunch, but you're the only one whose swimsuit has a zippered pocket. You don't want your friends losing their money in the water and then begging you for food, so you place everyone's money into your high-security pocket.

Now you've got a new problem. If you don't keep track of how much money each person gave you, and how much they spend at lunch, at the end of your wet day you'll have no idea how much money to give back to each person. Or you may forget it's their money and accidentally pig out at their expense. To be smart, you write down all the amounts on a piece of paper so you can keep everyone's account straight. Of course, when you go swimming, the ink washes off, so you're back where you started. I guess this wasn't such a good analogy after all.

Your checking account is kind of like that pocket (but drier). All the money may be in the same place, but your GIVE ledger shows that some of that money actually goes back to God. If you didn't keep a separate ledger, you might accidentally spend the money, and that messes with your priorities. That's why you keep a separate ledger for this priority. Just don't go swimming with it.

The ledger comes in handy in another way. Let's say you earn money weekly but like to save up your giving and make one donation at the end of the month. Not a problem. With each new income deposit in your checking account, you also record 10% of your income as a deposit in the GIVE ledger. At the end of the month, you can write one big, fat check and record the donation as a withdrawal in your GIVE ledger.

SAVE ACCOUNT

This next priority is even easier. If your budget calls for you to put 20% in savings, then you've got to get $10 out of your checking account and stick it in your savings account. If both accounts are at the same bank, you can *transfer* the money from one account to the other. If not, you can write a $10 check to yourself and deposit that check into your savings account. Either way, you record the first step in your check register, and the second step as a deposit in your savings account register.

If you have a passbook account, the bank will record the savings account transaction for you; the passbook acts as your SAVE ledger. If not, you'll need to write the deposit on your own SAVE ledger, just like you did with the giving thing. But unlike the other account, the money in your savings account is indeed separate, so you won't accidentally spend it when writing a check. And if you're *really* smart, your savings account ledger will soon show hundreds of deposits and no withdrawals until you're ready to buy that car, house, jet, or college education.

SPEND ACCOUNT

I think you're getting this system by now, so I'll be brief here. After you've distributed your income to the GIVE and SAVE account ledgers, what's left gets recorded as a deposit in the SPEND ledger. When you make a

The number one, as a numeral or a word, appears 16 times on a dollar bill.

withdrawal by using your authomated teller machine (ATM) card or writing a check, you record the transaction in the check register *and* write it down as a withdrawal in your SPEND ledger. That way, you'll always know how much money you can afford to spend. If you just look at your check register (like most people do), you'll keep spending money you can't afford. Your SPEND ledger tells what's *really* available for spending.

NEW PRIORITIES GET NEW ACCOUNTS

This four-account system works just fine if you're living at home with your parents and don't have a lot of expenses. But what do you do if you're paying car insurance, rent, food and utility bills, or want to save some cash for a special one-time expense? It's simple: create new accounts.

Let's say you and your youth group are going on a weekend ski trip, and you need to come up with $200 to cover everything. First, you'll need to revise your budget. You're not going to steal money from these priorities just to go skiing, so the cash is going to have to come from your SPEND account.

Using that old budget as our example, you've got just $35 weekly to work with after meeting your giving and saving commitments. If the trip is ten weeks away, you'll have to set aside $20 a week. If you make your plans three months in advance, you can meet your goal by stowing away about $17 each week. Obviously, the more planning you do, the easier it is to attain your goals.

New Weekly Budget	
Income	+ $50
Giving (10%)	– $ 5
Saving (20%)	– $10
Ski Trip	– $25
Spending	= $10

Unfortunately, sometimes the problem isn't *your* lack of planning—it's someone else's. In this case, your youth group leader forgot to tell you about the trip until just eight weeks before it was supposed to happen. If you want to keep your bigger priorities and still make the trip, you're going to have to squeeze your spending to just $10 a week.

After you've written a new budget, you need to create a new ledger. Label it SKI TRIP. As with your other priorities, make a deposit in this ledger each week, keeping the money safe in your checking account. When it comes time to pay for the trip, you can withdraw the cash from your account without messing with your other priorities.

This same system works for your other expenses. If your car insurance comes to $800 per year, your weekly budget should show a new priority. You'll need to set aside about $15.50 a week and make a new account ledger. Of course, if you're living on your own, with monthly bills for housing, electricity, food, phone, medical insurance, and the dozens of other things you need, you'll drive yourself crazy and kill way too many trees if you create a separate ledger for each expense. You can avoid all that paperwork by consolidating expenses into categories:

- **housing:** rent, utilities, phone, purple beanbag chairs
- **transportation:** insurance, gas, maintenance and repairs, bus fare, limo rides
- **food:** groceries, restaurant meals, ice cream sundaes
- **personal stuff:** clothing, shoes, toiletries, make-up, anchovy toothpaste
- **fun:** CDs, sports gear, vacations, trips to Tahiti
- **taxes:** (sorry)

The SPEND account can get divided into lots of different categories. In fact, it doesn't really matter how many budget categories you have. Nor does it matter if you use a weekly or monthly budget. Many people, such as real estate brokers, big investors, (and authors), may get paid just once or twice a year, so they work with annual budgets to keep their priorities straight, the bills paid, and the accounts in order. You can even keep your money in those little envelopes if you don't want to mess with a checking account. I won't tell.

In other words, you can pretty much do anything you want to this money management system, as long as it works for you. After all, the whole point is to help *you* control your money so you can get the most out of it. Let's review the two big steps:

1. Make a budget based on your priorities.

2. Keep your budget with separate accounts.

Simple, simple, simple. The next move is yours. What are your priorities? Do they show in how you handle your money? Without even knowing you, I can predict your future—If you can handle this simple system and make a habit out of it, you're going to have more fun, accomplish greater things, avoid more misery, and have a bigger positive impact on our world than 90% of the people on this planet.

This bright future starts right here, right now. Make your move.

In 1995, Americans spent over $46 billion at the dentist's office.

Yep, Taxes

As your income grows, so will the government's interest in your earnings. Fortunately, you won't have to mess with tax forms till you either make a fair chunk of money, or move out on your own. For example, in 1997, if you live at home and make less than $4000, you don't need to file a tax return.

However, if you're working a real job and your employer withholds taxes from your paycheck, you'll want to fill out and mail in a tax return form because you're likely to get most of that withheld money back! That's because the government doesn't expect you to pay income tax until you make a semi-decent income. Until then, you can consider the withholding tax as a forced savings account. It doesn't earn interest while it's safe with Uncle Sam, but at least you can't spend it till you get a refund check.

There are all sorts of exceptions and tricky rules about who needs to file a tax return and how much tax you're likely to owe. If you're paying withholding tax at a real job, be sure to talk to a wise parent or boss or teacher about it. One of the duties of living in this big, fine country is helping to pay for its upkeep. But you're never obligated to pay more than your share.

Chapter 5

Get a Checking Account

In the last chapter I told you that a checking account acts as your INCOME account, and also serves as a safe holding tank for your GIVE and SPEND accounts. If you have regular income, a checking account is a great way to go. This chapter explains where checking accounts came from and how they work right now. If you don't need a checking account right now, you can skip this chapter. Otherwise, follow me on this quaint little history trip.

YOUR BUTLER'S BANK CHECK

Simply put, a check is an *IOU note* from you to the person you write it to. Originally, checks were just handwritten notes: "Dear Bank of Biff: Please give my butler, Bernard, $100 from my account." Bernard would take the signed note to your bank. The

25

bank teller would check the signature on the note to see that it matched the one in your file and give Bernard the cash.

To make things easier, banks now print up standard forms for these IOU notes with your name and account number printed on each note. These standard check forms save you from writer's cramp. What's more, they make it possible for banks to honor each other's checks. Now Bernard doesn't have to trudge down to *your* bank to get his money—he can cash the check at his own bank.

Your bank and his bank (and everyone else's bank, for that matter) have an arrangement. When Bernard's bank cashes that $100 check, they send the check back to your bank and ask for the money. When your bank receives that well-traveled check again, they deduct $100 from your account and send it your butler's bank. Then they send you the canceled check as a receipt for the money they took out of your account. Everybody is even. Until you bounce a check.

A check bounces when your bank tries to deduct the money from your account, but there's not enough in there to cover the amount on the check. They send a reply back to Bernard's bank, saying, "Sorry, we can't pay you the money." So Bernard gets a call from *his* bank, saying, "Give us back that $100 we gave you." Bernard gives back the cash, then yells at you for bouncing his paycheck. This time you pay him in cash.

THE REAL STORY

Now that we've got this whole check-swapping process laid down, let me tell you a few other details. First of all, most banks don't really exchange the checks directly with each other. Instead, they use their own bank accounts at the Federal Reserve Bank—that's the bank for banks. Each bank has an account there, and that $100 gets deducted from your bank's bank account and deposited in your butler's bank's bank account. That's a little more confusing, which is why I left out this detail in the story. It doesn't matter—it all comes down to the same thing: sooner or later, that check makes it back to your bank, and the money gets withdrawn from your checking account.

Sometimes this process can take a day; other times it can take a week or more. However long it takes, this time period is called the *float.* The float is the delay between the moment a check is written and the moment the money is deducted from your checking account. Some people use the float as a sneaky (and illegal) way to pay for things when they don't yet have the money. For example, if you knew that it took five days for the banks to process a check, you could write your butler a check on Monday, even though you won't have money in your checking account till you get paid on Friday.

That's a dangerous way to do business. If the banks manage to process the check on Thursday, you're caught. If you've done this sneaky trick before, Bernard will get smart and cash the check at *your* bank, which eliminates the float altogether. In either case, you'll bounce the check and get charged a fee for your misdeed. After you've bounced a few checks, your bank will get fed up and tell you to take your business elsewhere.

The float causes one other big problem, and it occurs when you *reconcile* your checking account. Each month, your bank sends you a statement listing all the transactions they handled in the previous month—deposits, withdrawals, checks cashed, fees, and so on. If you write a $100 check a few days before the end of the statement period, the check may not get processed until after the statement is printed. Your check register may show that you've got, let's say, $50 in the account. But the statement shows that you've got $150. You figure that you must have made an error in arithmetic—after all, banks are professionals at math; they *must* have it right. So you spend your $100 windfall.

A few days later, that $100 floating check lands at your bank . . . and bounces. The bank charges you $25 for your stupidity. Ouch.

RECONCILIATION

To help you avoid bouncing checks, banks print little reconciliation worksheets on the backs of their statements. When their statement shows a different balance than the one in your check register, you flip the statement over and fill out the worksheet. It shows you how

to account for uncashed checks, missing deposits and withdrawals, and pesky fees that you didn't record.

Many people think that reconciling a checking account is too much work. But if you can handle a few simple additions and subtractions, the worksheet on the statement is a piece of cake. Do it every month, and you'll avoid bounced checks, painful fees, and upset butlers.

By the way, some checking account transactions have little or no float. Electronic banking allows you to "write" checks on your computer or phone. As soon as the bank computer receives your data, it deducts the money from your account and electronically transfers it to the account of the *payee*—the person or company you write the check to.

If you use an ATM card to pay for gas or groceries, the bank does the same thing—the money is instantly deducted from your account. The same is true with a debit card. These things look just like credit cards, but they work like ATM cards. When you swipe a debit card through a magnetic reader and enter the amount, the bank immediately debits your account. In each of these cases, there's no float.

MONEY MANAGEMENT

If you understand the float and take a few minutes each month to reconcile your register with the bank statement, you'll find that a checking account is a great way to manage your money. Let's see how that bonehead-easy management system works with your checking account:

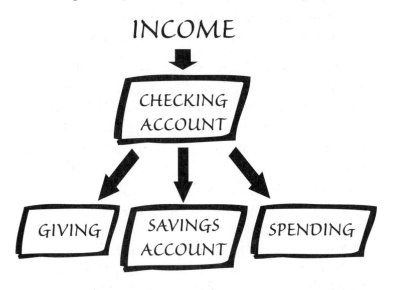

INCOME

CHECKING ACCOUNT

GIVING — SAVINGS ACCOUNT — SPENDING

1. INCOME: *Deposit* all income in your checking account and record the transaction in your check register.

2. GIVE: Record a portion of that income as a *deposit* in your GIVE ledger. Look at your budget to determine the percentage. The money stays in your checking account, but you know what it's *really* for.

3. SAVE: *Transfer* a portion of that income to your savings account. Again, your budget will tell you the percentage.

4. SPEND: Record a portion of that income as a *deposit* in your SPEND ledger. To calculate that amount, just subtract your giving and saving amounts from the income you just deposited.

Now you're set. If you need spending cash, withdraw it from your checking account, and record the transaction in your check register *and* your SPEND ledger. Remember, some of the money in your checking account is already earmarked for giving. Your check register shows *all* the money. Your SPEND ledger shows you what you can really spend.

The same thing works for your giving. When you write a giving check, record the transaction as a withdrawal in your check register *and* your GIVE ledger. Every check gets recorded in two places: the check register *and* the ledger you're taking the money from.

It'll take you a few weeks to get used to this system. So what? Once you have it wired, you'll have a foolproof system for tracking all your money, and you can use it for the rest of your life. Add new SPEND accounts by creating new ledgers. And when you start dealing with tens and hundreds of thousands of dollars, just make the ledger columns wider!

With this system you can have a few priorities or a dozen. You can track a minimum wage income or a million-dollar salary. And you can do it all by starting with a plain old checking account.

The U.S. Census Bureau estimates that the American 12-to-19 population will grow to 35 million by the year 2010.

Part Two

Making Money

We just finished talking about how to manage your money through four basic accounts: INCOME, GIVE, SAVE, and SPEND. These four accounts give us the four topics covered in the rest of this book. How to:

Make money (INCOME)

Give money

Save money

Spend money

The next few chapters are all about making money. For most of us, making money means getting a job. I'm about to show you how to find and land a good job, how to get the most out of that job, and even how to start your own business. Read on.

Get a Job!

For most teenagers, finding a job isn't a problem. It's finding a *good* job that takes effort. In this chapter I'll show you how to find *that* kind of job. It's done in three steps. But before we take those steps, we need to consider all the things that a job can do for you.

The first thing is obvious; it pays money. That's a good thing and the reason we're even talking about jobs in this book. But jobs pay other dividends besides money; some good, some bad, and some downright ugly. Let's look at each in turn.

THE GOOD PARTS

First, let's take a look at the good parts—the great rewards of working a good job:

- It pays money. Your paychecks fund your INCOME account, which in turn funds your GIVING, SAVING, and SPENDING accounts. All good.

- It shapes the way you perceive work. A good experience now will make work in the future better. Since you'll probably be working for the next 40 to 50 years of your life, it's nice to start off with a healthy perception.

- It can do wonders for your self-image. It's a good feeling to know your boss and coworkers depend on you to do a job that you know you can do.

- It exposes you to new people—good and bad. You may find yourself getting along great with people you'd never have picked as friends. Suddenly all your "rules" about who's cool and who isn't, don't apply.

- Unlike much of what you learn in school, the things you learn at work are put to use immediately. You don't learn things because you'll be graded on them, but because you need to.

- You may do such a good job that your boss makes you vice president with access to the company jet and a condo on Maui.

Your first work experiences are test drives. From these early jobs you'll learn what you like and dislike about certain kinds of work and what you want to do in the future.

That's what happened with two teenage ambulance drivers way back in World War I. In the midst of their gruesome tasks these two guys would talk about what they wanted to do when they got older. They dreamed about the kinds of businesses they'd start, how they'd manage them, and how they'd treat employees. After the war these kids went off to do what they planned. Ray Kroc bought a little hamburger stand from the McDonald brothers and made McDonald's a household name. His buddy, Walt Disney, drew mouse cartoons and built Disneyland. Their early job experiences changed the rest of their lives and impacted the rest of us.

JOBS GONE BAD

While some teenage jobs can be great, others don't always turn out so well. Before you take a job, you better look at the potential bad stuff:

- If you work too much during the school year, your education is going to suffer. Working late on school nights is the best way to sleep through your first two classes.

- If you spend all your time at school and work, your family may forget your name (clue: your Christmas gifts are marked, "To Occupant").

- You may lose valuable time for friends, sports, church, music, or other important priorities. (But if you have no friends, hobbies, or personality, a job will do you good.)

- Working after school each day will prevent you from watching endless *Saved by the Bell* reruns.

Studies show that high school students who work more than 20 hours a week are much more likely to do

It's the Law

Jack London (the guy who wrote *The Call of the Wild* and *The Sea Wolf* and lots of other great stories you really ought to read) had some tough jobs as a teenager. At age 15 he worked 10 hours a day in a cannery for $1 a *day*. At 18 he shoveled coal 12 hours a day, 7 days a week with one day off per month. His wage: $30 per month.

Nowadays, things are a bit better. To protect you from some of the hazards of overwork, the government has laws about how many hours you can work and the types of jobs you can do. The Fair Labor Standards Act is the federal law affecting anyone under 18. It says that you can't work during school hours or perform dangerous work, such as operating meat-slicing machines, working up on scaffolding, painting tigers' toenails, etc.

If you're under 16 the above restrictions apply, plus a few more: You can't work more than three hours on a school day, work past 7:00 P.M., or put in more than 18 hours during the week.

Each state has its own labor laws, which may be stricter than the federal law. Although the federal law doesn't require you to have a work permit, your state may. You can get the facts from a school counselor or librarian, or by calling the employment or labor office listed under the State Government section of the phone book.

37

poorly in school, develop nasty habits like drinking, smoking, and abusing drugs, and generally mess up their lives far beyond what the bigger paychecks can fix. And even if you manage to keep up your grades and morals, your family life may take a hit. Parents who are overeager to see their kids working often regret it when family time suffers. You're the best influence in your kid brother or sister's life. Too much time at work means not enough time for the ones who need you most.

AND NOW FOR THE UGLY PART

Working long hours at an unpleasant job can do more than use up your time and energy; *it can make you cynical about work in general.* The job may become a necessary evil that you're willing to tolerate only until you can afford to quit it. Unfortunately, many of the jobs available to you can turn out that way. *Don't think, just push these little buttons, take the money, give back the change shown on the computer screen, and say 'Have a nice day.'*

It's true. Some of your friends are working in jobs that may pay well, but cost far more in damage to their education, family, friendships, and self-image than the fattest paycheck can compensate for.

FINDING A GOOD JOB

Before you run off and find yourself just any old job, you've got to do some homework. You must make

certain that your job won't mess up your life. That brings us to the first important step in finding a *good* job.

Step 1: Count the Cost

The decision to work is a great one. Take it seriously. Look at all the factors—not just the paycheck. Here's your homework assignment:

- Consider how many hours you can afford to work without doing damage to your other priorities.

- Talk to friends who have jobs. Find out what they're learning—and what negative effects the jobs have had on their lives.

- Look at who you are and how that will affect the kind of job you might like. Are you an introvert or extrovert? Organized or spontaneous? A team player or lone ranger? An early bird or night owl? Frantic or methodical? A job that doesn't complement your personality can make you miserable.

- Talk to your parents. You can work for the next 50 years if you want to, but you'll never buy back the time you'll lose with your family.

- Pray. Your *real* Boss has a perspective on your life and future that no one else can see. Ask God what's best for you. He may have other "jobs" for you right now that don't pay money.

If you determine that a regular job isn't right for you at the moment, that's great! If you believe that a job would be a positive addition to your life, that's great too. But the decision has to be yours. Count the cost before you decide.

Now you've got three options for reading on:

- *Option 1:* If a regular job is too expensive, you can skip the rest of this section and move to chapter 12, which starts the section on giving money. Chances are you've got an allowance and odd jobs bringing in some cash, so you still have some money to manage. As your personal situation changes, you'll find other work opportunities. You can read the rest of this chapter then.

- *Option 2:* If you've already got a good job that isn't harming the rest of your life, you can skip to chapter 8, "Keeping Your Job."

- *Option 3:* If you don't have a job right now and have determined that you should still get one, then read on. The next two steps will help you find one that matches your priorities.

Step 2: Write a Résumé

Now we can move on. You've considered your options, counted the cost, and are ready to hunt down a good job. Start by putting together a résumé—a summary of your most important work and educational accomplishments. At this point in your career you may be asking, "But what if I don't have any?" You do. And one reason why you should write a résumé before going out to look

for a job is to show *yourself* how accomplished you are.

The first résumé you write is intended for your eyes only. Don't plan on handing it out to potential employers. Its purpose is to convince you that you've had valuable experiences that will help you do any job better. Here's how to write a résumé that works even if you've had little or no formal job experience.

LIST YOUR JOB EXPERIENCES

Make a list of all volunteer or paid jobs you've had, no matter how small or insignificant they may seem. Under each job, identify the main responsibilities and accomplishments. Here's an example:

Personal Résumé

Delivered Newspapers
delivered papers every day: solicited new subscribers, got few complaints, trained my replacement

Baby-sitting
baby-sat for 8 different families on regular basis: considered reliable by parents, well liked by kids

Concession Stand Sales
worked snack trailer at Little League: sold food, worked cash register, cooked on the grill, set up the soda fountain

School Newspaper Reporter
reporter for junior high newspaper: wrote one article per week; interviewed principal, teachers, and students; learned editing, layout, printing, and collating

---

IDENTIFY YOUR SKILLS

These jobs won't astound any potential employer. But they should convince you that you have work skills that make you very hirable. Points to discuss in an interview might be:

- *works under pressure* (Little League concession stands are mob scenes after a game)

- *reliable* (the paper route and baby-sitting show you that)

- *teachable* (learning new skills such as how to set up the soda fountain at the concession stand and editing the school paper)

- *can teach others* (training your replacement with the newspaper route)

- *sales experience* (concession stand and newspaper route)

MEASURE YOUR ACCOMPLISHMENTS

What's lacking in the above list is any measure of *how well* you did. So go back through it and try to quantify as many accomplishments as possible. As a newspaper deliverer you increased your route size 30% in three months by selling new subscriptions and got awarded on three occasions for zero-complaint months (don't mention that in another month you hit one cat and broke two windows).

In the baby-sitting department, you averaged five requests a week and baby-sat for one family over 50 times. At the concession stand you personally served up to 40 customers in one hour (and killed 12 cockroaches). And at the school newspaper you figured out a way to cut the printing and collating time in half.

Each of these numbers works as *evidence* to back up your skill claims. Anyone can say they work well under pressure, but you've got the numbers to prove it.

PUT IT ALL TOGETHER

You're beginning to look like Super Worker. Now rewrite your work skills using your *measurable* work experience to support your claims. It might look like the résumé on page 45.

Of course, this isn't a final résumé; your school library has books showing how to lay out the rest of the document. But those book examples may not show you that your work experience, no matter how small, can be conveyed in ways that highlight the skills employers are looking for. Employers already know you don't have a lot of experience—that's what they get when they hire teenagers. What they're looking for is someone who can take what he or she already knows and use it to learn more. Listing your job skills in this way shows them you can.

What's even better, it shows *you.* After reading your list a few times, you should be convinced that you have great strengths and important work skills. And if *you're* convinced, you stand a good chance of convincing a potential employer.

If you're applying for a sales clerk position and the manager asks you if you've ever worked in a store before, you can reply, "No, but I've had some sales experience. I've worked at a baseball concession stand, handling as many as 40 customers in an hour; and I've sold newspaper subscriptions, increasing my paper route by 30% in three months. I know how to make customers smile, and I'm pretty good at what to do when they're not happy." That sounds more impressive than telling her that you sold hot dogs at a baseball game and got people to subscribe to the newspaper.

Lots of people say that you should print typed copies of your résumé onto nice paper and give them out to potential employers. For many adult jobs, the résumé is essential. But when you're a teenager looking for work, it's not as important. Indeed, some experts believe that if you don't have lots of job experience, there's no point in handing out a half-empty sheet of paper that proves it. Many employers go through stacks of applications when they're filling a position and may not have time to read résumés.

Whether or not you should hand out copies of your résumé is a decision you'll have to make for yourself. To help you, ask some of your working friends what they've done. If your parents have friends who employ teenagers at their workplace, you might also ask them what's best. The job-hunting ideas listed in the next step don't

Get a Job!

Work Skills

Work Under Pressure
Concession stand sales: regularly served up to 40 customers in one hour
School newspaper reporter: consistently met tight weekly deadlines

Reliable
Baby-sitting: many satisfied families, including one that hired me over 50 times
Newspaper delivery: awarded for zero complaints three months in a row
Concession stand sales: handled cash register, kept inventory and orders

Teachable
School newspaper reporter: learned all aspects of editing, layout, and printing

Can Teach Others
Concession stand sales: trained one new employee per month
Newspaper delivery: trained my replacement

Sales Experience
Newspaper delivery: increased route size 30% in three months

require a résumé. If you think one is necessary or help-ful, go ahead and publish one. But remember: the résumé's most important task is to convince *you* that you've got what it takes to get a good job.

Step 3: Go Hunting

Armed with a clear idea of what you want from a job and what skills you can bring to it, you're ready to begin the hunt. Oops, not quite. First I need to give you a big fat warning.

Big Fat Warning

If you look around town and see stores and fast-food joints with big NOW HIRING *banners in their windows and job applications print-ed on their place mats, you're likely to fig-ure that finding any old job is easy. And you're probably right. But you're not look-ing for any old job.* You're looking for a GREAT job—one that fits your schedule and priorities and teaches you skills that will count in your future. *Don't rush out and take the first job that comes to you. Hunt for the best job in town.*

Get a Job!

Okay, now that we've gotten that out of the way, let's look at the best ways to find the best job. About one-fourth of all employees find their jobs by applying directly with the employer. In other words, they just walk into the store or office and ask about a job. Sometimes they do so in response to a sign in the window. But don't let the lack of a HELP WANTED sign stop you. Like most things in life, the best job is not always advertised.

The best way to shop for jobs door-to-door is to pick your doors in advance. This is the fun part. Ask yourself, "If I knew that just by walking into any business I could get hired immediately, which business would I choose?" Chances are, you'd choose a business that was close to home or school, looked like a nice place to work, and dealt in something that interested you. That last part is important. Which businesses match your career dreams, interests, or hobbies? Make a short list of your ideal employers—those that fit your needs and dreams.

Now you've got a job-shopping list. Stop by each of the places on your list and ask about a job. Dress in the kind of clothes you'd wear on the job, but a little nicer. At each business, walk in and ask to speak to the manager. (If she's not in, ask when she'll return, then come back later.) When you meet the manager, smile, introduce yourself, and ask if you can apply for a job. "Hi, my name is Carl Brown. I'm a student at Central High School and I'd like to apply for a job."

Minimum wage in 1960: $1.00 per hour.

Your introduction line says a mouthful about you. You're direct, confident in who you are and what you do, and you're ready to talk business. Believe it or not, you've just made a better presentation than 90% of the job seekers she's met. She's probably heard "Yeah . . . um . . . I'm looking for a job," a hundred times and will be surprised and impressed. She may be so impressed she'll hire you on the spot.

Of course, there's also a good chance that she won't. Maybe she has no positions available. If she says so, ask if you can fill out an application anyway, "in case something opens up." Again, you've made an important statement: You're serious about working for her. That puts you in the top 5% of job applicants. The others just say "OK" and walk out the door.

This next part is a bit tricky, so pay attention. If the manager *is* hiring and seems interested in you, sit down and fill out the application as neatly as possible. If you don't do it now, the job may not be there when you come back. If the manager is not looking to hire someone right away but she's willing to give you an application anyway, tell her you'd like to fill it out at home and bring it back the next day. *If you don't know her name, ask her for it.* Then thank her *by name* for her time and move to the next business on your job-shopping list. Right about now she's thinking that she'll never see you again. Students have an often undeserved reputation for not following through. You're about to surprise her again. More on that in a moment.

Help Wanted

Here are some of the most popular part-time jobs available for teenage workers year-round:

- cashier
- child-care worker
- retail salesclerk
- stock handler, bagger
- kitchen assistant
- janitor, maid
- food counter worker
- construction worker, framer
- waitress, waiter
- restaurant host, hostess
- secretary, typist, data entry clerk
- painter
- receptionist
- shipping or warehouse worker
- mechanic
- service station attendant
- nurse's aide, orderly
- computer operator

First things first. As soon as you're out the door, be sure to write down the manager's name and the day's date. Also check to be sure the name of the business is on the application. If it's not, use a sticky note or light pencil to mark the name on the application. You're about to collect several such applications, and you'll look silly if you turn in the wrong form to each business.

When you're done job shopping for the day, go home and fill out each application very neatly. If you've decided to use a résumé, staple a copy to the back of each application.

Now it's time to make *another* strong impression. The next day, go back to each business to turn in the application. Ask to speak to the manager again. When you greet her, do so with the same honest confidence you used before: "Hi, Ms. Jacobson, I'm Carl Brown. I stopped by yesterday. Here's the application you gave me." Translation: You're *thoughtful*—you remembered her name; you're *polite*—you saved her the awkwardness of trying to remember yours; and you're *reliable*—you said you'd be back with the application, and you were right. You've just graduated to the top 2% of all teenage job applicants.

The manager still may not be able to hire you, but you can bet that your name will stand out among the other applicants she's met. Think of it this way: If you walked into a room filled with strangers, then spotted a person you barely knew, chances are you'd head straight to that person, almost like you were old friends. To a manager flipping through a stack of job applications filled out by complete strangers, you at least look like an acquaintance. She'll head straight for your phone number.

And even if she doesn't, you've made strong impressions with several other managers who just might.

If your extra work comes to nothing—that is, no one calls to offer you a job—you've got another chance at the businesses on your job-shopping list. After a week has passed, stop by again. Introduce yourself again. Politely ask if any positions are opening up. Most teenage jobs have a high turnover rate. Workers quit on short notice to take other jobs, leaving their employers scrambling for replacements. The manager *not* hiring last week is suddenly desperate to find someone this week.

The employers you met several days ago may now be ready to fill a position. And as we just discussed, they'll be more likely to hire someone they barely know over a complete stranger. Believe it or not, if it's been a few weeks since you applied, they may not bother calling you, figuring that someone as sharp as you surely got hired somewhere else. Stop by and let them know you're still interested.

If your door-to-door job hunt turns up empty, you may want to make a new list. Broaden your search to other businesses that may not be as ideal but still match your priorities and interests. As I said before, finding the right job may not come easily. But when you consider the amount of time you'll spend at work and the impact your job will have on your life, you'll remember why it's important to get the best job you can.

Of course, the door-to-door method is not your only hunting weapon. Here are other proven job-finding methods:

CONNECTIONS

I'm sure you've heard people say, "It's not *what* you know, but *who* you know." Many times, that's true. If an employer has a choice, he'll hire someone he knows (or at least someone who knows someone he knows) before hiring a complete stranger. That means the best way to look for a job is not in the want ads, but among your family and friends. Ask your parents if they have any friends who might be able to help you find a job where they work. Ask your own friends about open positions at their jobs. If your friend is a good worker, her recommendation is worth a lot (and if she's a sloth, you may be getting *her* position).

TRADING PLACES

If you have a friend who is getting ready to quit a good job, you may be able to take his place. But the employer will do this only if your friend is a good worker. If not, she won't respect your friend's opinion of other potential workers. You'll still have to sell yourself to the boss, but you've already got one foot in the door.

If your friend has a sensational job that's hard to get, make the deal more enticing to the boss. Offer to let your friend train you for free. Work alongside him without pay during his last day or two. You'll make it very easy for the employer because she won't have to go through all the trouble of searching, interviewing, hiring, and training. (If you happen to look a lot like your

friend, you can do the switch without even telling the boss! But when payday comes, it may be tough to cash the check!)

SOURCE SEARCH

You already know about the newspaper want ads. But there are other job listings available to you. The chamber

---

A Working Summer

Here are some popular summertime jobs for teenagers:
- lifeguard at a pool, lake, or the ocean
- swimming instructor
- state or county fair worker
- day camp counselor
- recreation assistant at a community park or recreation center
- amusement park worker
- worker at sports equipment rental at a beach or lake
- camp counselor for the Boys Club, Girls Club, YMCA, or private camp
- maintenance or kitchen help at a summer resort
- farmhand
- dockhand at a marina
- pool or beach assistant at a resort, country club, or yacht club
- sports coach for a summer sports league

---

of commerce in your city may list summer job opportunities, as may your school's career center or counselor.

The Labor Department's U.S. Employment Service has offices in many cities throughout the country, which list jobs in the area. You can call them by finding the number in the government section of the phone book.

Many YMCAs, churches, and other community organizations sponsor job boards listing part-time and summer jobs open to teenagers. Get out the phone book and call as many of these organizations as you can locate. Even if they don't have a job board, they may be looking to fill a job for which you qualify.

COLLEGE JOBS

Employers who can afford to pay higher wages for part-time help will go after college students, whom they hope will be more reliable and mature than younger students. To attract college students, these employers often advertise on job boards at the local college or university. Most schools have a bulletin board or office that posts positions of interest to students.

Make a visit to the school and get the information on any openings you're interested in. Visit each potential employer. Introduce yourself just as we covered earlier, but be sure to mention that you read about the job at the college. If you follow the same method, you should be able to prove you're as reliable and mature as any college student they're likely to hire.

54

Money

Get a Job!

Minimum wage in 1980: $3.10 per hour.

WORK FOR FREE

Some jobs are worth going through drastic measures to get. Lots of students are willing to take an unpaid internship just to get a foot in the door. If you're a hard worker, and a paid position eventually opens up, you're in the ideal place for it.

The best way to get an internship is to talk to teachers and other adults who may know employers in your desired field. For example, your art teacher may know a graphic artist who's looking for an assistant.

If you have no connections, go directly to the employer. Explain that you're willing to work for no pay in exchange for the training and experience. Make it clear that you would like to be considered for a paid position if you prove your worth and a job becomes available. If the employer senses that you're sincerely interested in the opportunity and not a vulture hovering around until someone quits, dies, or gets fired, she may take you on.

SOONER OR LATER

We've covered a lot of ideas in this chapter. Before we move on, let's review the important steps:

- *Step 1: Count the Cost.* Talk to parents, friends, and God. Determine if a regular job can deliver what you need without messing up your other priorities.

Minimum wage in 1990: $3.80 per hour.

- *Step 2: Write a Résumé.* Its most important task is to convince *you* that you've got what it takes to get a good job.

- *Step 3: Go Hunting.* Make a list of your ideal employers, then go and introduce yourself. Make a good impression and keep impressing. If nothing turns up, broaden your search.

Depending on the job market, you may land a job on your very first try, or you may have to keep hunting for weeks and weeks just to get an interview. If you don't meet with immediate success, keep at it. As I said earlier, teenagers tend to change jobs suddenly and often, forcing employers to find replacements in a hurry. Keep looking at job listings and continue to make your door-to-door visits. Sooner or later you'll be in the right place at the right time, and someone is going to need what you have to offer.

There are two more steps to landing a good job: the *interview* and the *job offer.* These are big steps, so we'll save them for the next chapter.

56

Money
Get a Job!

Minimum wage in 1998: $5.15 per hour.

Take a Number

One of the things you must give an employer before you're hired is a *social security number.* This is your official "account number" with the U.S. government, which they use to track how much money you've put into your social security account. When you get old and retire, or if you become disabled before that ripe old age, you're entitled to social security *benefits*—typically monthly checks that can supplement your income someday. Nowadays, most parents apply for a social security number for their kids soon after they're born. If your parents were buried in dirty diapers and forgot to apply for you, now's the time to do it.

It's easy: Look for the number of the *Social Security Administration* in the government listings in the phone book. If you call them, they can send you an application by mail. And if they have an office near you, you can apply in person.

Chapter 1

Job Interviews
and Offers

Most adults must go through a job interview before getting
hired. Some teenagers have it easier. The high turnover rate in
teenage jobs forces employers to fill positions quickly, sometimes
without a formal interview. A desperate employer may conduct
an interview like this one:

BOSS: Are you human?

YOU: Yes.

BOSS: Are you an escaped convict?

YOU: No.

BOSS: You're hired.

But if you want a *good* job, you'll have to go through a
more thorough interview. Typically, the better the job, the
tougher it is to get—and the more important it is for the
employer to pick the right person. That's why you'll go through
an interview. Think of it as a sales pitch. The product you're
selling is *yourself.*

Advertisers know that if their ad doesn't grab the reader in that first second or so, he won't bother to read any further. An ad that fails in the first second is a failure—*regardless of how good the rest of the ad is or the quality of the product it sells.* Now imagine that you and everyone else looking for a job are just advertisements in a magazine. The employer is flipping through the magazine very quickly deciding every moment whether to read an ad or turn the page.

Fortunately, if you've managed to meet the boss face-to-face, you have more than a few seconds to make your impression; you have an entire minute! In that first minute, your potential employer is going to make some important decisions about you. Here's how to make every second count.

BEFORE THE INTERVIEW

You can do a lot to improve your interview before it even starts. Before you go in for your big chat, find out as much as you can about the business. If it's a big company, it's probably listed in one of the corporate directories at the library—ask the librarian where to look. You can also call friends who've worked there. The more you know, the more intelligent you'll sound during your interview. It will also be obvious to your prospective employer that you care enough to do some homework.

It also may help to write out a list of questions you have about the job responsibilities and expectations and the company in general. The answers will help you decide if the job is right for you.

REHEARSE

Practice answering the questions the employer is likely to ask. Have a friend or family member interview you using these questions so you can get comfortable talking about yourself. This will also teach you how to answer questions *succinctly* (that means short and sweet). Here are some questions you may be asked:

Tell me about yourself.
Make it short and sweet; your school, grade, family, interests.

What subjects do you enjoy? Why?
Be honest; show enthusiasm for things you like.

Sports? Hobbies? Other interests?
Again, show enthusiasm and a sense of dedication for the things you care about.

Do you drive? Own a car?
What he's really asking: "Can you be counted upon to get here on time?" and "Can you run errands that require driving?" If you don't have a car, assure him that you have a reliable means of getting to work.

What are your strengths?

What he *wants* to hear: "I work hard, learn fast, and I'm reliable." If it's true, say it.

What are your weaknesses?

"Acceptable" weaknesses are those that amount to too much of a good thing: perfectionism, too task-oriented, overly self-critical.

What are your future plans?

Anything ambitious sounds better than "I don't really know."

What days and hours can you work?

Have a copy of your schedule; be honest about *non-negotiables*—school, study, church, family time.

Why do you want to work here?

Good place to work, challenging, nice coworkers, good reputation, quality product—whatever is true.

DRESS

Wear what you'd wear on the job if you were hired. If you're unsure, it's better to overdress than underdress. But make sure you feel comfortable—if you *feel* strange, you *look* strange.

GROOMING

It's not just for dogs and cats and horses anymore. It's important for humans too:

- Fix your hair so it stays out of your eyes. Compulsive adults will be thinking of how to shove it out of the way for you.

- Don't wear a lot of cologne, perfume, or after-shave. (Hint: If they smell you before they see you, it's too much.)

- Try not to smell like tobacco, gasoline, or a wet dog.

- Get the cat hair off your sweater.

- Remove the Milk Duds debris from your teeth.

- Avoid makeup that looks like it was applied while you were riding on a motorcycle. This is especially important for girls.

- Use a breath mint.

ARRIVE EARLY

One of the things that employers hate most is people who don't show up on time. Arriving early may not win you any points, but showing up late is a major strike against you. Don't do it. Before you step through the door, make sure your hair, face, teeth, and elbows are in order. Bring a notepad and your questions with you. Also bring along an extra pen; a mean-spirited federal statute (hustled through Congress by the pencil lobby) requires pen manufacturers to design their pens in such a way that a certain percentage will run out of ink in the middle of a job interview. Or so it seems.

While you're waiting for the interview, casually look around and see if any of the workers are watching you. If one employee seems to be staring, it's probably because she's afraid she is about to be fired and you're going to get her job. *What do you have that she doesn't? Why are you so special?*

You wish you could tell her not to worry: you're not interviewing for her job. But how do you know that— maybe you are. No, the manager said it was for a "new" position. But of course that's what he has to say. He doesn't want her to know she's history until he's hired a replacement. What if you are her replacement? No wonder she's sneering. Maybe she hates you for it.

Or maybe she hates you for another reason. Maybe she's thinking you're not here for a job at all. The "interview" story is just your cover—you're an undercover detective hired to prove that she was the one who embezzled the $5,000. Is she starting to sweat? Does she rub her wrists, wondering what the handcuffs will feel like?

Oh, no—she's reaching into the desk drawer for something. What is it? Scissors! She's coming for you! You plead with her: "Look: I don't know anything . . . I'm just here for a job—not your job, someone else's—don't hurt me!"

"I'm not going to hurt you . . . you have a loose thread on your shirt; sit still, and I'll get it for you."

THE BIG CHAT

If you survive your imagination and make it into the interview, here's what's next. Your object is to convey as many of your positive traits as you can before bringing up any negatives. Sell yourself. You've got two pitches, really: how you act and what you say. Let's look at each.

HOW YOU ACT

Actions and gestures speak loud in the first few seconds of a conversation—often louder than the words themselves. Here are some body language tips and what they declare:

Gesture	Translation
Offer to shake hands when you meet—age and gender don't matter. Give a firm, friendly grip, look into the person's eyes, and smile.	*Meeting you is important to me.*
Look directly at the person's face when you speak.	*I believe in what I'm saying.*
Do the same when you're listening to people.	*I care about what you're saying.*
Don't put paper clips in your nose.	*I can be trusted with office supplies.*

Money

How to Make a Lousy First Impression

- Ask: "How long do you think it would take me to get *your* job?"
- Tell her all the times you're not available.
- Bring along a friend and insist that hiring you is a package deal.
- Bring your grandmother with you.
- Trim your nails.
- Ask if you can smoke a cigar while you're meeting.
- Eat an anchovy sandwich immediately beforehand.
- Tell her the family picture on her desk reminds you of a trip you took to the zoo.
- Point and say "Nice tie!" Then laugh very loud.

WHAT YOU SAY

Your ability to communicate is being evaluated. Speak in your normal voice. When you greet the person, always give your name. If she has forgotten it, you'll save her the embarrassment of having to ask. (And when you repeat it, you make it less likely that she'll forget again.)

As a general rule, address an adult by his or her last name (e.g., Mr. Rogers, Ms. Piggy, Dr. Jekyl) until you're given permission to use the first name. Use the name frequently—people like to hear their names. And above all, don't use swear words unless you have a note from your mom.

Remember that you're selling yourself. In the few minutes you have, let the interviewer discover that you're someone special:

- Convey what makes you unique. You want to be remembered.

- Show interest in the job, not the compensation.

- Employers don't expect teenagers to be experts when they hire them. They're looking for *enthusiasm, eagerness to learn, a cooperative spirit,* and *reliability.* If you can convince the interviewer that you possess these attributes in your interview, you've done the best you can.

- Every interview is a priceless lesson: take notes, *learn from your mistakes,* look back and laugh, and get better.

- Never start a water balloon fight during a job interview (but if someone else throws the first balloon, go for the kill).

When you feel it's appropriate, ask your own questions. The kinds of questions you ask will tell the manager a lot about you: You're smart, not afraid to ask questions, and interested in the job. Jot down a few notes on the answers—if you're the least bit nervous in the

interview (no big deal—most people are), your notes will help you remember the important stuff that's said.

Try not to bring up hours, vacation, pay, and benefits until the end (unless, of course, the interviewer brings them up first). It's helpful here to have a copy of your weekly schedule including school hours, regular obligations after school and evenings, and weekend commitments. If it's a complicated schedule, you may want to give a copy of it to your interviewer. If you've sold yourself well in the first part of the interview, your future boss may be more flexible with these things.

Sometimes an employer is ready to hire you after the interview. If not, don't fret. He or she may have scheduled other interviews, or may need to talk to a bigger boss before making a decision. If no offer comes, ask when you might expect to hear an answer. Then smile and thank the person with a handshake.

JOB OFFERS

After an interview, send a thank-you letter to the person who interviewed you. If there was more than one interviewer, write the note to the one who has the power to hire you. Mail the letter that day so the person doesn't have an opportunity to forget you. Now continue your job search, meeting managers and lining up interviews—keep working at it. Your goal is to have at least two or three offers to choose from.

When you get a job offer, generally by phone, thank the person sincerely. Write down the details; starting date, wage, hours, and so on. Tell the employer that you'd like to accept but you need a day to discuss it with your family. Now talk it over with your parents and some close friends. Compare the job offer to your original goals. *Sometimes in the excitement of landing a job you can lose sight of your own best interests.*

If you applied elsewhere and prefer that position over the one you're being offered, you may be able to use the offer as an incentive to get a quicker decision from the other employer. Call or stop by your first-choice employer. Explain that you got another job offer but would rather work for him. If he turns you down, you can accept the first offer. If he offers you the better job, then you're set. You have a job either way, and you can be confident that you got the best deal available.

Of course, that trick works only if you *get* an offer. What if no one calls? Unless the employer has specifically told you not to, it's appropriate to call back in a week to find out if there's any news. If the position is still open, it gives you one more opportunity to be heard from; if it's filled, you can move on. If you've done this right, you have several other businesses considering you so you can continue to pursue them.

HANDLING REJECTIONS

Okay, here comes the painful part—rejection. No matter how wonderful you are, you're going to be rejected many times in your life. It may not happen the first time you look for a job, but sooner or later, you'll get turned down. There are a hundred reasons why you'll get rejected for a job, and most are *beyond your control.* Here are a few:

- The employer got a tax bill and realized she couldn't afford to hire anyone.

- She once had a terrible worker with the same name as yours, so she subconsciously ruled you out.

- An old employee wanted her job back, which was easier than training someone new.

- The manager was forced to hire the owner's nephew, Winthrop.

- Your application got thrown out by mistake.

- Something in your manner reminds her of her Uncle Hubert, whom she can't stand.

- She called your number twice; the first time there was no answer, and the second time it was busy, so she went to the next applicant.

- Your personality rubbed her the wrong way.

- You looked too smart to be satisfied with such a low-paying job for very long.

69

Lots of times the employer can tell you wouldn't be right for the job. She understands her business, knows the kind of workers that fit best, and may know that you'd be miserable working there, even if you don't see it that way. These kinds of rejections aren't fun, but in the end you're happier because of them.

Then there's the bad sale. Sometimes you don't get the job because you conveyed the wrong message. Here are top reasons employers give for not hiring student workers:

- poor personal appearance
- overbearing, know-it-all
- poor communication skills
- interested only in paycheck
- wants too much too soon
- makes excuses, is evasive

- lack of interest
- lack of tact
- lack of courtesy
- lack of vitality
- little sense of humor
- lazy

If you come off in one or more of these ways during an interview, you'll need to work on fixing the problem. Every interview is a lesson in selling yourself—something you'll have to do for the rest of your life. Learn from your mistakes, and do a better job next time.

No one likes rejection. *No one* is immune to its pain. It cuts some people deeper than others, and lots of folks are experts at smiling on the outside while they're dying on the inside. When you've been rejected, it's okay to "let it get you down" (despite what everyone is so quick to advise). Just know that the quickest way to stop feeling bad is to go back out there, give a winning interview, and land a exciting job.

70

THROUGH THICK
AND THIN

Let's end all this talk about rejection. The fact is, if you're smart enough to read this book, you've got what it takes to get hired. Every new fast-food place, shopping mall, and retail store needs part-time workers. They don't need people with years of experience; they can't afford to pay the salaries of such people. They need *you:* part-time, with minimal experience and a desire to work hard and learn as you go.

As I write this, the economy is growing, businesses are expanding, and many of these businesses are desperate for workers. That means you can afford to be choosy. Shop around for the best job you can find.

One of these days, the economy will slow down (what goes up, must come down), and that may be the case as you read these words. It doesn't matter, because even in a tight market, with few businesses hiring new workers, you've got what it takes to find a good job. In fact, the steps and skills I've shown you in this chapter are even more important in a tight job market. When the competition for jobs is high, you must excel to land a job that's right for you.

Through thick and thin, big and small job markets, you can succeed in finding the job that matches your priorities. And when you do, you'll want to *keep* that great job. That's what the next chapter is all about.

Salary means "salt money," from the days when Roman soldiers were given money to buy salt to preserve their food.

How to Look Older

If you look young for your age, here are some things you can do to age yourself:

- Dress more conservatively.
- Walk slower, stand taller.
- Pause before speaking.
- Make fewer gestures; don't talk with your hands.
- Wear a fake mustache (most effective with guys).
- Remove the Chiquita Bananas sticker from your forehead.
- Don't come in holding your mom's hand.

Chapter 8
Keeping Your Job

True confession: I've hated every job I've ever had . . . for the first month. The first days in a new job are miserable; I forget everyone's name, and when I do remember, I get them mixed up—"My name's not Ralph—it's Rebecca!" I become so self-conscious that I not only forget everything I've just been taught but everything I've *ever* been taught: multiplication tables, how to tie shoes, and the whole concept of opening the door *before* I attempt to leave the room.

But the condition is only temporary. After the first month I become normal again (relatively speaking) and start to enjoy the job.

Most employers understand that your first few weeks may be rough, and they generally cut you some slack. But there comes a time when you had better do your job right; if you want to keep it, you'll have to deliver.

It's one thing to get a job. *Keeping* it is another. Some of the smartest people I know have lost good jobs because they didn't deliver what the boss really needed. Others have managed to keep their jobs, only to waste away their days in boredom or misery because they didn't take advantage of their situation. How can you get the most out of *your* job? How do you get promoted? Get raises? Resolve conflicts? How can you learn so much that the boss can't afford to replace you? I've got some job-saving answers for you, including more "insider information" from boss-type people.

LEARN EVERYTHING YOU CAN

Most teenagers think the only reason they're working is to earn money. While the paychecks are nice, they're just one of many rewards. One of the greatest rewards is *what you learn.* So if you're not learning everything you can while in that job, you're making a lousy investment of your time and energy.

Whatever your job, there's important and helpful stuff to learn there. Even a seemingly brainless job like operating a cash register in a fast-food place is rich in learning opportunities.

Learn how the food-dispensing machines work— and what to do when they break down. Observe how the different kinds of customers order things. What part of the display menu do they look at first? (When you open your own fast-food place someday, you'll want your best items advertised where the customers are most likely to look first.) How do they decide among the choices?

What prompts them to order a special deal? What's the average amount spent by teenagers? construction workers? people wearing business suits? moms with their preschool-aged kids? How often does the little toy in the kid's meal make or break the sale?

How full can you stuff the napkin dispenser before people get thoroughly frustrated and grab a giant chunk? What kinds of people leave their trash for someone else to clean up? What kinds of cars do they drive? How did these slobs ever graduate from kindergarten?

Sometimes this knowledge is practical. Just as often, it's not. But it's still *valuable*—it teaches you to be a better observer of the people and things around you. A sharp mind and quick eye will take you far in this world.

The thing that prevents most people from learning is their own stubbornness. For example: Every time the photocopier jams, Sandy has to ask someone else to fix it for her. Her excuse is always, "I'm not mechanically inclined." She can drive a car, use a computer, and dissect a cat in biology, but she refuses to learn the few simple steps to clearing the copier's paper path.

There's nothing wrong with not being mechanically inclined. Just don't apply for jobs repairing jet engines or designing oil refineries. But in most jobs available to you now, the simple and complex tasks are conquerable *if you're willing to try.*

Make a list of tasks being performed where you work, from loading receipt paper into the cash register to reordering merchandise from a supplier. If your normal responsibilities are covered, pick something off the list and ask someone to teach you. Think of it this way, unlike school, you're actually getting *paid* to learn. Grasp every opportunity to do so.

Quick story: When I was nineteen I worked in a small hospital. One day both the cook and his assistant went home sick. In two hours there would be 120 people waiting for their dinners, so the supervisor began a frantic search among the staff to find a cook. I volunteered. (I'd cooked scrambled eggs before, and I knew how to heat up soup.)

I read the menu plan, switched around some things that were too difficult to prepare, and started cooking. I made a few calls to friends for answers to important questions (how to put out a grease fire, how to make the chef's hat pouf out at the top). I served the meal on time, everyone was happy, and they asked me to do the next meal too. A few years later I handled the meals for my own youth camps—something I had the confidence to do because of that experience. Now when I cook, people say it tastes like hospital food. I don't know why.

On-the-job learning pays other big dividends. It keeps you from getting bored when things are slow. The next time you complain of boredom at work, take on a task that you're not familiar with. Read a manual, figure out how a machine works, ask your supervisor if he's tired of doing something and volunteer to do it for him. Once you've learned something, you can teach others what you know. If you're good at it, you're in the best position to get a promotion.

The best advantage to learning is that it provides job security. The more you know, the more difficult you are to replace. Learn so much that your boss could never afford to lose you.

DO WHAT'S RIGHT

Your job is one of the toughest proving grounds for your integrity. Behavior that's clearly wrong at home or among friends is often standard conduct at the workplace. Work is where many people who disapprove of lying, cheating, and stealing have no problem calling in sick when they aren't, stretching the hours on their time cards, or taking home merchandise that's not theirs.

Behave according to what you know, not according to the code of ethics that you see others following.

That's not easy. In lots of jobs, it seems impossible *not* to cheat. The problem with cheating is that it's so habit-forming—it's a thrill to rearrange reality to suit your tastes. And the thrill that you're getting something for nothing is delightful, because you can remember so many times when you got nothing after working your tail off. But if you cheat enough, trying to cope with life "as is"—without rearranging the facts—becomes a real chore. And it doesn't take long because cheating is a strong drug.

It's true: cheaters *do* prosper. But amazingly enough, so can honest people. Maybe not as fast, or as great, but honest people attain their goals without sacrificing their character. Sometime in their lives most people stop being consumed by how far they're going and pay more attention to *how they're getting there*. Do what's right. You'll get where you're going and enjoy the trip along the way.

GIVE THE BOSS A BREAK

Most bosses are easy to please. In many businesses employers have put up with so many irresponsible workers that one who simply shows up on time makes employee of the month. Here are five traits that bosses *really* value in the ideal employee.

1. PUNCTUAL

Showing up late, leaving early, and failing to come at all are among an employer's biggest headaches. When you're supposed to be there but aren't, either work isn't being done or people more responsible than you are taking up the slack. If you think changing your habits to get to work on time is tough now, wait until you're twenty-five or thirty and that habit is as much a part of you as your name. It's now or never.

Show up five minutes early every day. Every week that you have a perfect attendance record, treat yourself to a frozen yogurt or some other reward. Don't call in sick unless you're sick. Nobody likes being lied to. If you've agreed to work that day, do it. If you'd like a day off, plan ahead—get someone to work for you and work it out with your boss.

2. COOPERATIVE

Almost every job is a team effort. It doesn't matter how well you work if you can't get along with others. Sometimes being a boss is like being the referee of a professional wrestling match—employees gossiping, backbiting, fighting, and occasionally dragging *them* into the skirmish. Play fair, do your best to get along with others, and follow directions. You'll be a hit.

3. TAKES INITIATIVE

When it comes time to work, lots of people go into *robot mode.* The boss tells them to do something, and they do it. But that's all they ever do. If the boss himself doesn't tell them what to do, they stand around with a blank look on their face. Obeying your boss is important, but it's not enough. Act like a *human.* Take some initiative. Decide for yourself what must be done, then do it without being told.

Make a list of the things your boss tells you to do. The next day, do them all before he has a chance to tell you. When you've mastered that list, make a new list of things you *haven't* been told to do, then ask if you can take on those tasks too. If your boss is one of the few on this planet who don't like workers who take initiative, don't worry about it. Just let *his* boss see your initiative, and you might end up being the boss yourself.

4. HONEST

Lying about the number of hours you worked, giving out freebies to your friends, helping yourself to merchandise without permission—it seems like everyone does these things. Not quite everyone. There actually are a few honest people left, and they refuse to lie, cheat, or steal. Be among them. As a Christian, you have a Boss that expects nothing less. Remember who you really work for—and let your actions show it.

5. ENTHUSIASTIC

On the job there's one thing worse than being unhappy: being the boss of someone who's unhappy. If you have any reason to be excited about your job, let it show. Enthusiasm is contagious. The goal is to contaminate everyone near you.

Make a game out of it. On your way to work each day, ask yourself what you can look forward to. Come up with something—*anything*—that's worth getting excited about. If you really want to test your enthusiasm skills, think of the worst, most boring, most dreaded task you'll encounter that day, and figure out how to make the task exciting. The truth is, if a task is absolutely awful, you've got nothing to lose. Laughing, smiling, whistling about it cannot possibly make it *worse*. Surprisingly, it often makes it better.

JOB REVIEW

Some bosses conduct job reviews to evaluate your work and give you suggestions for improvement. That's a good

thing, but it's not nearly as important as the review you give yourself. Open your calendar and mark "Job Review" on the first day of each month. When review day comes, sit down and evaluate your work. Rate yourself on your success in these three areas:

1. *Learn everything you can.* Are you doing it? Make a new list of things you don't know. Learn them this month.

2. *Do what's right.* Have you been working that way? Where have you cut corners? Examine your work habits and make sure you're doing everything with fairness, honesty, and integrity. If you've failed somewhere, admit it, repair it, and commit to what's right.

3. *Give the boss a break.* Would your boss say you've fulfilled your responsibilities and exceeded her expectations? What will you do this month to go beyond what you've done already? Make new goals. Get to it.

Most folks consider their jobs as something they *have* to do. It doesn't have to be that way for you. Work each day like it's something you get to do. Your job can be a treasure of rewards that develops your knowledge, social skills, integrity, initiative, and self-discipline. The paycheck is just the bonus.

Chapter 9
Things You Can Do to People When You're the Boss

Here's what I'm picturing: You worked hard to land a *good* job. Once there, you worked even harder, proving yourself as the ideal employee. In fact, you've done such excellent work that your employer has now made you a boss. New title, new responsibilities, (hopefully) new money, . . . and the power to tell other people what to do (get my coffee, shine my shoes, do ten push-ups).

Actually, you probably already know that being a leader is mostly what you do *for* other people—not *to* them. If you want to grow in your job and be as good a boss as you were a lowly worker, you'll have to work harder than ever. Here are five ways to be a good boss.

1. BE FAIR

Each of us has a built-in justice meter—it instantly tells us if we're being treated unfairly. If we sense any kind of injustice against us—favoritism, backstabbing, partiality, discrimination—

a red light in our brain starts blinking, and we cry out, "That's not fair!"

If you're an unfair boss, most workers will hesitate telling you; they fear that you'll attribute their complaint to jealousy on their part, rather than favoritism on yours. Instead, they'll hold grudges, gossip and complain to each other, and fight with each other to attain your favor. It's a big mess.

If you're a fair boss, workers will stop worrying about "getting what they deserve" and concentrate on doing a good job. OK, so you'll still have a few problems from workers with tweaked justice meters. You can't have everything.

When you're the boss, people count on you to uphold justice. That's a full-time job because injustice can creep in anywhere. Pay attention to the following areas.

PRAISES

If someone does something right, praise her. But if two people are worthy of praise and you neglect one of them, you're being unfair—and the neglected person knows it. It's like when your mother praises your little brother but fails to see much good in you. After a while, you just give up trying to please her and turn your attention toward putting your little brother in the clothes dryer. That strategy doesn't work on the job site (unless you happen to work at a laundry). Be quick to praise your workers—but make sure that you're praising *all* who deserve it.

83

HOURS AND POSITIONS

Some people are professional manipulators, always getting the hours they want without alerting you to what they're doing. When you make decisions on jobs and hours, do so with a list of everyone in front of you. You'll be able to spot whether someone always seems to get a much better deal.

LOOKS AND DRESS

It's true—the good-looking people of the world get the most attention. It's not a romantic thing, just human nature. They're more pleasant to be around so you give them more of your time, attention, compliments, help, and kindness. If you want to be a fair boss, pay close attention to your attentions. Affirm people for who they are, encourage them in what they do. Forget what they look like.

2. BE BIG

As a kid, if I found a scary bug in my room that I was too frightened to kill, my dad would always come in and do the job. He never cleaned my room or made the bed, but he could be counted upon to squash the scary bugs. Now I have my own house, and I can't call him up for an execution anymore (OK, I tried once, but the bug crawled away before his plane landed). It's my job now; it comes with the territory.

84

When you're a boss you've got to be big sometimes. People are looking for a leader, and you're it. That means squashing bugs, stopping fights, making impossible decisions, and fixing other people's mistakes. That's one of the reasons why you're getting paid more than they are. Look around you and try to find some tasks that won't get done unless you're big enough to do them.

3. BE REAL

There are two voices in your brain. The first says, "If I admit my mistakes, I'll look weak and lose people's respect." The second says, "When a person I respect admits her mistakes, I end up respecting her more." Isn't it amazing how you can know a fact but think you're the only one on the planet that it doesn't apply to?

When you're wrong, say it. It may temporarily streak your self-image, but it polishes the image others see.

Let's say you lose your cool and ridicule a worker in front of everyone. A moment later you regret your action and decide to admit you were wrong. You can say you're sorry in two ways. No matter what words you use, the first kind of sorry means, "I'm sorry because what I did made *me* look foolish." The only thing you regret is the damage you did to yourself. Let's call that a *selfish sorry.*

The second kind of sorry means, "I'm sorry because I embarrassed *you,* hurt *you,* and didn't treat *you* with the

85

respect *you* deserve." You realize, regret, and admit the damage you did to the *other* person. Let's call that a *proper sorry* because, well, that's the proper way to do it. You don't need to tell someone which sorry you mean— she knows from the *way* you say it. When you're the boss, stick to the proper sorry.

4. BE NICE

It's hard to get through a day without getting hit by a negative remark from a teacher, coach, friend, or family member. Some days you start to wonder if there's a note on your forehead: "Rip on me—I like it." You can give your coworkers an oasis of praise in an often cruel world. Here are some nice things to say and do:

Affirmation is declaring what's true. You affirm someone when you tell her what's true about herself— "You're a punctual person," "You think clearly under pressure," "You juggle chain saws better than anyone I know." Since most of us are frequently reminded of what we *aren't*, it's a real boost to hear good things about our talents and qualities.

Your affirmation will carry twice the power if you show the person proof of your claim—"I just saw how you handled that angry customer. You were quiet, friendly, and showed her that you cared. When it comes to dealing with customers, you're a pro." She can't deny it—you've got her pegged.

Encouragement literally means "to fill someone's heart

with hope." Long hours, a tough workload, problems with coworkers—these things and a hundred more can discourage people on the job. You can give a little hope with a kind word, a smile, a round of M&Ms, or a pat on the back. One of the best encouragements is to pitch in and help someone get the job done.

Appreciation is thanking someone for what she's done for *you.* "Thanks for carrying the box—you saved me an extra trip." "You make my job much easier. I appreciate your hard work." "Thanks for squashing that bug—my dad's stuck in traffic."

Get in the habit of writing notes. A spoken praise is often forgotten, but a short note of affirmation, encouragement, or appreciation makes it official—you mean what you say.

5. Be a Servant

You've probably seen an organizational chart. Companies often use these to show who's the boss of whom. In most organizations, the chart looks something like this:

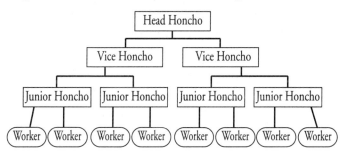

A few companies flip the chart. They put the big boss at the bottom and the minimum-wage workers near the top. The customers go at the very top of the chart.

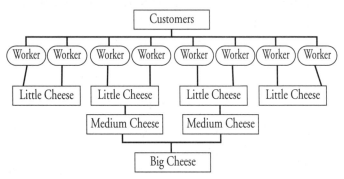

This upside-down organizational chart makes a big statement: the customer comes first. The workers are the next level down—their job is to serve the customers. The bosses are arranged beneath them, with the task of serving the workers. This goes on all the way down the chart.

Your employer may use the first or second chart, or no chart at all. It doesn't matter to you. In your *mind,* take the people you manage and put them *above* you. That makes you the *servant* of the people you supervise. Your job is to do what it takes to make them happy, excited, and effective in their jobs.

Like a butler, a good boss-servant anticipates the needs of those he serves—and meets those needs before being asked. Train people so they can do their jobs better. Treat them fairly so they can concentrate on customers instead of worrying about petty grievances. Praise them so they can feel good about themselves and their work. And every once in a while, serve them tea and biscuits on a silver tray.

THE BIG BOSS

In the previous chapter I said that Christians work for a Boss named God. No matter what kind of job you have, ultimately, you're working for him.

In the first section of this book, I pointed out that God is the owner of everything in this world, including the money we call our own. We're just the managers. We get to manage God's money.

The same is true with people. When you're a boss, you don't *own* the people who work for you. Your workers are ultimately owned by God—you're just managing them for him. That's a BIG responsibility. God has strong opinions on how people should be treated.

Fortunately, he doesn't just tell us how to act, he shows us. Jesus was a living example of how to manage people. If you want to be good boss, act like Jesus.

1. *Be fair.* Jesus is the definition of justice. It's not some abstract idea he invented—justice is who he is. On earth, he treated everyone with fairness. He avoided favoritism. He

demonstrated justice in everything he did. As a boss, you must do the same.

2. *Be big.* Jesus did lots of great stuff when he showed up on this planet, but his greatest act was dying for our sins. No one else could do it. Thank God he was big enough to do it for us. As a boss, you won't be asked to die for your workers. But you will be asked to do things that are unpleasant, unfair, or painful. Being a boss means that you're big enough to do them.

3. *Be real.* Jesus took off his royal robes, left his plush heavenly estate, and came down to sinful, smelly earth to show us how to live right. He was perfect, yet he didn't let that stop him from being a real human that other real humans could relate to. As an imperfect boss, you must be willing to show up as a real human that your workers can relate to. Real humans fail. When you fail in front of your workers, confess it.

4. *Be nice.* Jesus wasn't merely fair, he was merciful. He comforted those who were feeling discouraged. He praised the good things they did. When people made the right choices, he affirmed them for their actions. Jesus celebrated what was right, best, and true. As a boss, you must do likewise.

5. *Be a servant.* Above all, Jesus was a servant. Every day, in every way, he placed himself last. Everyone he encountered, no matter how small or unworthy, was more important than himself. As a boss, you must set aside your own needs and look after the needs of others.

Here's the best part. As you act like Jesus on the job, your coworkers will begin to see glimpses of him in you. As a Christian, and especially as a Christian boss, your greatest success will come when others see evidence of the real Boss in you. They'll figure out who you *really* work for. And just maybe, they'll want to work for him too.

Chapter 10

How to Quit and
How to Get Fired

A job can be a great thing to have, but sometimes it also can be the last thing you need at the moment. Every semester you need to *recount the cost*. Ask yourself the same question we asked earlier. Do the job pressures and conflicts, as well as less time for studying, friendships, family, church, and other activities, outweigh the benefits of the money and experience? If so, it's time to quit.

Of course, there are plenty of other reasons to quit. Maybe the problem is not holding down a job, but keeping this particular job. Some work conditions are intolerable:

- You have an unresolvable conflict with a boss or coworker

- You're forced to work under unsafe conditions

- You or your employer is doing something you believe to be immoral or illegal

- Coworkers are having a negative influence on your behavior or attitude

- You're being sexually or physically harassed
- You've found a job that suits your needs better

Whatever your reasons, carefully write out all of the positive and negative aspects of the job. The next time you look for a job, review the list so you can avoid getting yourself into a similar situation.

GOING OUT IN STYLE

Once you've made the decision to quit, you've got to tell your boss. If you're a bad worker, she may leap for joy and be so excited about being saved from the trouble of firing you that she won't even bother to ask for a reason.

But if you've been a good worker, she's likely to demand a reason for your decision to quit. Know your honest reason before she asks or else you might get talked into staying, or start an argument, or wind up saying something you'll regret. (As you'll see in a moment, you don't want to make an enemy of your soon-to-be former boss.)

If you're quitting because of the money, tell her so—but be ready for the possibility that she'll offer you more. If you've found a better job, tell her you think you would be happier at it. If the reason the new job is better is beyond her control (e.g., closer to home, related to your career interests, better hours), let her know so she won't feel personally responsible. If your reason for quitting is to spend more time with family, friends, school, or church, say so.

However, if the *boss herself* is the reason you're leaving, be careful what you say. You're not obligated to give a reason for your decision, especially if that means saying negative or hurtful things. If that's the case, and she demands a reason, just tell her that the other job will work better for you. Arguing about her weaknesses isn't your responsibility. A nasty confrontation could jeopardize a good recommendation and cause her to take out her anger on other employees, especially those she knows are your friends.

When you state your intention to leave, let her have two weeks' notice to give her time to find a replacement. However, just because you *give* her that much time, it doesn't mean she has to *take* it. She may find it more convenient to have you leave immediately. Or she may keep you on until you start *acting* like you're leaving, working with an "I don't care anymore" attitude. If you want to work for the next two weeks—and get a good recommendation for your next job—you're going to have to work hard.

HOW TO GET FIRED

If you're just too shy to say, "I'm quitting," here's some good news—you don't have to say it. Through careful planning, you can irritate an employer to such an extent

that he actually tells you to leave. Here are some behaviors to help him make up his mind:

POWER TARDIES

Determine how many minutes late you should arrive by raising the number 10 to a power equal to the number of days played until you're fired:

Day 1: 10^1 = 10 minutes late
Day 2: 10^2 = 100 minutes late
Day 3: 10^3 = 1,000 minutes late (16 hours, 40 minutes)
Day 4: 10^4 = 10,000 minutes late (1 week)
Day 5: 10^5 = 100,000 minutes late (69½ days)
Day 6: 10^6 = 1,000,000 minutes late (2 years)

SALAD BAR BRAWL

If you work in a restaurant with a salad bar, post yourself at one end of the bar, armed with a long set of tongs. Watch customers to make sure they don't drop broccoli bits in the potato salad or spill ranch dressing in the low-cal French. If someone makes a mess, use the tongs to tweak him on the nose. If he still refuses to clean it up, dump his plate out and send him to the end of the line. Should a customer complain to your boss, start a food fight. Open fire with croutons and three-bean salad; cut down the enemy's visibility with clouds of cottage cheese and crumbled-up hard-boiled eggs. Now make for the door, pouring oil-and-vinegar dressing across the entrance to foil a pursuit.

BOSS FOR A DAY

Quietly lock your boss in the supply closet when no one is looking. Tell the other employees that he had to leave the country for an indefinite period—and he's appointed you as the new boss. If anyone objects, fire her. Give raises to the people you like, and schedule the next employee meeting for tomorrow . . . in the Bahamas. Call the travel agent, book the flights, and use the petty cash to buy Bermuda shorts and black socks for everyone.

GRACIOUS DEPARTURES

Given the two choices—quitting and getting fired—it's best to choose to quit. Make every effort to depart with your boss as a friend. Write down your reasons for leaving, then review that list as you consider new job opportunities. If your next job suffers from the same drawbacks, you'll be right back where you started. That's no fun.

We've got one more issue to cover on the topic of jobs: starting your own business. If you're interested, go to the next chapter. If not, you can skip all that stuff and move to the next section, giving. Take your pick.

Chapter 11
Starting Your Own Business

Teenagers go into business for themselves for lots of reasons. Some want the flexibility that comes when *they* set the hours. Others want a job that's more challenging than what most employers can offer. Some start their own business because they can't get anyone else to hire them. Lots of students think they've got a great idea and want to go for it.

Whatever your reason, starting a business is scary, exciting, and lots of work. There's no way we can cover everything in just one chapter; a proper discussion on this topic would require its own book. If after reading this chapter you think you have what it takes to start a successful business, check out other books on the topic at the library or bookstore. Find out all you can before you decide to take the plunge.

FIND A NEED AND FILL IT

Every business is an example of someone discovering a need and getting paid to fill it. For example, people need more food than they can raise in their own gardens, so *grocery stores* fill the need. Cars burn up the gasoline that was in the tank when you bought it. *Gas stations* fill the tank. Parents sometimes like to go places without their children but can't leave them running loose at home. *Baby-sitters* provide the solution.

Because of changes in the economy, technology, and people's lifestyles, new needs are being created all the time. Here's an example.

Once upon a time, people needed machines that could juggle big stacks of numbers and work faster than an adding machine. Someone invented the *computer*. Then people needed to share information between computers, so someone came up with *networking*. When people wanted to connect computers that weren't in the same building, *modems* were invented, and eventually, the *Internet*. Then came fancy computer graphics that could be transmitted over phone lines, spawning the *World Wide Web*. That invention created a need for *Web-page designers*.

A few years ago, if you had advertised yourself as a Web-page designer, people would have had no idea what you were talking about. Now just about everyone knows what that means, and some of those people may be looking to hire you.

Here's my point. Successful entrepreneurs become successful because they've *found a need* and they've figured out how to *make money filling that need*. Whether it's an old need (people need their lawns mowed) or a new need (people need Web pages), if you can find a way to make money at filling it, you'll be a success. At

the end of this chapter you'll find a list of the big needs people have today—and how you might make money by filling them.

MAKE IT PAY

Any need-filling idea might make a great business. Then again, maybe not. It's not enough to find a need. You've got to figure out how to make money at it.

That's not so easy. Many people get all fired up about their brilliant business ideas. They have visions of customers lining up at their door, throwing wads of cash at them. They spend their savings buying equipment and advertising. Then reality sets in. The phone doesn't ring, people don't want what they're selling—and those who do want it aren't willing to pay what's needed to keep a business afloat. This sad scenario plays out thousands of times a year. Over half of business start-ups fail within the first year.

Entrepreneuring is tricky business. It takes vision to start a business, but if you have too much vision and not enough down-to-earth business smarts, you may start something that just won't work. What's more, vision and business sense won't get you anywhere if you're not willing to work your tail off. Successful entrepreneurs have a rare combination of imagination *and* plain old business sense *and* the drive to keep working when anyone else would call it quits. They've got one foot in dreamland and the other foot on solid ground—and both feet are in high gear.

vision + business smarts + drive = success

After you've dreamed up your wonderful business idea, test it with some real-world questions. Let's walk through the questions using a sample business. One of the business ideas I've listed at the end of the chapter is called Dog Gone Walking—daily walking and optional weekly washing for neighborhood canines. This is a pretty simple business idea, which is why I picked it. But whatever your business idea, you must ask these important questions.

1. RESEARCH YOUR MARKET

Don't just *imagine* your customers—find out who they really are, what they really need, and what they are really willing to pay. For your dog-walking business, you'll need to talk to as many dog-owning neighbors as you can. Does your idea sound good to them? Would they consider hiring you if you were to offer this service? How much would they be likely to pay?

Your business idea may look great in your head, but if it doesn't look good to *them,* your venture is likely to fail.

Dog Gone Walking: Weekly Income	
Daily walking service:	
$15 per week x 8 dogs	$120
Weekly washing service:	
$3 per dog x 9 dogs	$ 27
Total Weekly Income	$147

Money

2. FIGURE OUT WHAT IT WILL COST

You've probably heard the expression, "It takes money to make money." That surely applies to starting your own business. There are all sorts of ways to figure expenses, but we'll keep it simple for this example. The first kind of expense is called *start-up costs*—what you must spend just to get the business rolling. In the dog walking and washing business, you'll need *equipment* (leashes, grooming brushes) and *advertising* (flyers, newspaper ads, a big banner pulled by a plane). You'll need to pay for these things before your business brings in its first dollar.

Let's call the other type of expense *ongoing costs*—the regular expenses you must cover to stay in business. In this case, you have *supplies* (doggie treats, shampoo, lots

Dog Gone Walking: Start-up Costs	
Equipment	
2 good leashes	$ 30
grooming brushes	$ 20
Advertising	
flyers	$ 25
Total Startup Costs	$75

of bags for cleaning up "dog logs"). In many businesses, you may also need to pay for a *phone line, insurance, business permit,* and more *advertising.* Not to mention *taxes.* And most of all, you'll need *personnel*—chances are, that means just you.

This last expense is the one most people forget. They figure that the profits of their business will be their paycheck. It's exciting to learn that your business made hundreds of dollars last month—that is, until you add up your time and realize you made $2 an hour! Starting and running your own business takes lots of time—time that you *could* be spending at another job. Estimate the amount of time your business will require, then multiply that by the hourly wage you *could* be earning if you weren't working for yourself.

Most folks underestimate the true cost of starting and running a business. If you forget to consider something on your list of expenses, you could doom the venture to failure even before it starts.

Dog Gone Walking: Ongoing Costs

Supplies (weekly)	
dog treats	$ 4
shampoo	$ 3
dog log bags	$ 2
Personnel (weekly)	
$6/hr x 10 hrs	$60
Total Ongoing Costs	$69

3. ADD THE NUMBERS

Your market research should give you an idea of the number of likely customers and how much they're likely to pay. Your carefully considered list of needs will tell you how much it's likely to cost to satisfy these customers. Now add it all up. Income minus expenses will give you your bottom line. That's your *estimated* profit. Remember, if you include your own paycheck in the expenses, the profit is above and beyond your paycheck. Consider it a bonus.

Dog Gone Walking: 12-Week Budget

Income ($147 x 12 weeks)	$1764
Expenses	
start-up costs	$ 75
ongoing ($69 x 12)	$ 828
Profit	$ 861

4. ADD THEM AGAIN

Smart entrepreneurs spend lots of time working with these numbers and typically come up with at least three scenarios: worst-case, probable-case, and best-case. The worst-case scenario uses pessimistic figures—few

Dog Gone Walking: 12-Week Budget

3 scenarios

	Worst	Probable	Best
Income	$1044	$1764	$2200
Expenses			
startup	$ 100	$ 75	$ 65
ongoing	$ 934	$ 828	$ 988
Profit	$ 10	$ 861	$1147

customers, low income, lots of expenses. The probable-case version uses the figures you came up with above. The best-case scenario uses optimistic figures—more customers, higher income. In the best case, your expenses will probably be higher because you're working more hours and spending more on supplies. But, each scenario must be *realistic*—there's no sense in working up numbers for, let's say, a million customers. Save that scenario for when you're daydreaming in class.

As I mentioned, most people let their vision get the best of them, so it's pretty safe to say that your probable-case figures are already too optimistic. Pay attention to the worst case. That's likely to be a lot closer to reality.

Spreadsheets

If you're going to start a business, now is a good time to learn how to use a computer spreadsheet. Programs such as Microsoft Excel, Lotus 1-2-3, and Corel Quatro make it easy to manipulate columns of numbers for budgets and bookkeeping. A spreadsheet is especially helpful when you're running scenarios like the example above. Simply change a few of the assumptions (number of customers, average price, etc.), and the spreadsheet automatically recalculates the rest of numbers. You can run dozens of scenarios in minutes. And *bonus,* when your business starts making millions, you can widen the columns to fit in all those extra zeros.

5. COUNT THE COST

Wait a minute—didn't we just do that? Kind of. But the real cost you need to count isn't an arithmetic exercise. You must consider the cost to your nonfinancial priorities—school, family, church, friends, and future. As we discussed a few chapters ago, the time and attention you pour into your work can damage things that can't be replaced with cash. If the *true* cost is too much, set your plans aside. On the other hand, if you can start this new venture without sacrificing more important things, give it a go.

SELL, SELL, SELL

Launching a business is tough, but keeping it going is tougher. To survive, you must attract customers. Who are the people you'll be serving? How do you land them as customers? Basically, there are three circles of customers: 1) people you know, 2) people who know the people you know, and 3) strangers. Let's look at each circle.

CIRCLE 1: PEOPLE YOU KNOW

A few chapters ago I told you that the easiest way to find a job is to ask people you know. The same is true in finding customers. People buy goods and services from those they know and trust. That means your best prospects are family members, friends, and neighbors who already know you and trust you. That's your first circle of customers.

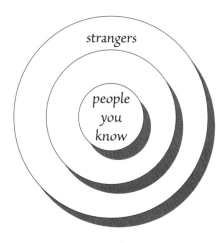

CIRCLE 2: PEOPLE WHO KNOW THE PEOPLE YOU KNOW

Chances are good that you won't muster enough customers from your circle of acquaintances—you'll need a larger circle. The best way to reach new customers is through word of mouth. That's how to reach the second circle—the people who know the people you know. If your current customers are thrilled with your work, they'll tell their friends. If they're *not* impressed with your work, they won't spread the word. (Or worse, they'll spread a *bad* word.)

That means that the quality of your service is your best advertising. Today's job well done is tomorrow's best advertisement. You'll keep hold of your current customers longer, and they'll help you find new ones. This is important in every business, but especially so in *your* business. The truth is, some folks are a bit skittish about hiring teenagers. Too many unreliable and mediocre young workers have preceded you on this planet, and you must overcome the unflattering stereotype they produced. When you consistently deliver good work at a fair price, adults are more than willing to discard that stereotype and tell their friends to hire you too.

CIRCLE 3: STRANGERS

It would be great if your business could survive in the first two circles, but most can't. You'll need to tap into that third customer circle: strangers. That's a big circle! There are several billion people on this planet who don't know you or your customers. That's OK—you probably don't want that many customers anyway. To find the customers you do want, you've got to narrow them down. Figure out who your most likely customers are (remember, the ones who really *need* what you're offering). Then figure out where you're most likely to reach these people. Now go there.

In that dog-walking business idea, your customers are dog owners who don't have the time or ability to walk their own dogs: they work long hours, or travel out of town, or can't get out of the house a lot because of a health problem or old age. Here's how you might reach them:

Potential Customers	*How to Reach Them*
People who work long hours	*Put flyers on doors, and company bulletin boards.*
People who travel out of town	*Tell local travel agents about your service.*
People who can't get out of the house	*Post flyers at senior centers, health clinics; post flyers door-to-door.*
Dog owners in general	*Post flyers at pet stores, at the vet's office; take out an ad in the pet section of the newspaper's classifieds.*

Sometimes your customers may find you on their own. For example, if you're walking down the street holding leashes on four dogs, some folks will figure that you're doing so professionally, and may stop and ask you about it. Make sure you've got flyers or business cards with you whenever you're on the job.

Of course, whenever you land and satisfy new customers, they move to that inner circle of people you know. Keep them happy, and they'll tell people in that second circle. To stay successful in your business, you must constantly move new people to that inner circle. You'll have to replace old customers that stop hiring you, and if you want to grow, you'll need more customers anyway. If you're *really* good, you'll get so many customers that you'll have to expand your business and hire some help. Then you can dream of opening a national chain.

As I said at the start of this chapter, there's much more to starting and running your own business than we can cover here. If you still want to dive into this great adventure, check out other books on the topic, talk to some small business owners, and learn everything you can. After all, it's *your* business. It pays you to do it right.

Big Needs and How to Fill Them

Here are some of the most common needs in our society, along with some business ideas that can fill these needs.

PEOPLE NEED THINGS DONE FASTER AND EASIER

Rent-a-Chef. Hire yourself out to neighbors and friends of your parents who don't have time to cook and clean up the dishes but would like an excellent meal prepared in their own homes.

Really Fresh Foods. Make your own peanut butter, apple pies, cookies, or candies, then package and sell them to neighbors and local stores.

Personal Shopper. Some adults are too busy to stand in line at the supermarket or drive all over town looking for a vacuum cleaner part. You'll take care of all their shopping needs at a certain cost per trip.

Go-to-Town Errands. Same idea, but you'll run any errand: pick up clothes at the cleaners, stand in line at the Deparatment of Motor Vehicles, take the dog to the vet.

KidLimo. Be a kid driver. Pick the kids up after school, drop one at the day care center, another at baseball practice, and take the third to the dentist.

Dog Gone Walking. For busy people with little time to exercise their dogs, offer memberships to your daily dog-walking service, with washing and brushing on Saturdays. Also offer pet-sitting to owners who go out of town.

All Sewn Up. Most people have a stack of clothes that need mending, altering, or just a button replaced. Offer door-to-door service.

Two Wheel Tune. Instead of hauling their bikes to the shop for tune-ups and flat repairs, your customers call you—you do the work at their home for less. Offer tune-ups, flat repairs, adjustments, and detailing. Offer to buy their old bikes; fix them up and sell for a profit.

Short-Order Servant. Hire yourself out as a butler, maid, server, or dishwasher for private parties. Advertise on bulletin boards where rich people hang out—tennis clubs, country clubs, or yacht clubs.

Friday Flowers. Sell once-a-week flower delivery to homes. Buy the flowers from a wholesaler, arrange them for each of your clients, and deliver them to their homes every Friday. Provide arrangements for their special occasions.

Wrap It Up. Offer in-the-home holiday gift wrapping. Customers provide the wrapping paper, ribbons, and tags; you put it all together.

Hired Pen. If you're a calligrapher, sell your penmanship to people who need to create or address invitations, Christmas cards, or name tags.

Other ideas. Gardening, lawn care, housecleaning, fish tank cleaning, window washing, pool cleaning, car detailing, auto maintenance, laundry and ironing, house-sitting, plant-sitting, Christmas light hanging, snow clearing, leaf raking.

PEOPLE WANT THINGS THAT BRING ORDER TO THEIR COMPLEX WORLD

Mr. Bills. Stop by your clients' houses once a week to organize their bills, write checks for them to sign, mail the payments, and file the statements. Balance their checkbooks each month, and organize their receipts for tax time.

Maximum Memories. Put together photo albums for people who take lots of pictures but never seem to have the time to organize them. Create scrapbooks for their children containing their art and schoolwork.

Proper Places. Organize peoples' kitchens, drawers, desks, albums, videos, files, offices, closets, pantries, and garages. Charge a fee for each area; offer package deals and monthly maintenance contracts.

I Haul. If you have a pickup truck (or can borrow one), offer to haul away garden debris, old appliances, and junk piles for a set price per load.

PEOPLE WANT QUALITY SERVICES FOR THEIR CHILDREN

KidCrafts. Put on crafts classes for neighborhood kids on weekends or during the summer. Print a flyer that tells parents what craft you'll be teaching each day and how much money the child has to bring to participate.

PlayCamp. Offer a day-camp experience for neighborhood kids at a local park. Do crafts, games, stories, and snacks.

Party Performances. Perform as a clown or magician for children's parties.

KidVids. Offer to videotape birthday parties, bar mitzvahs, recitals, plays, and sporting events. If you don't have a camera, see if you can borrow or rent one from school or a camera store.

Summer Girl. Hire yourself to a family as a nanny for the summer. Look after the kids all day during weekdays, with weekends off. If you don't want to work full-time, split the job with a friend by working alternating days.

Professor Tutor. Tutor kids in subjects you enjoy.

PEOPLE WANT GOOD SERVICE AT A REASONABLE COST

Formal Flowers. Sell dance corsages and boutonnieres to your classmates. Design several arrangements, take pictures, and use the photos to take orders. Get the flowers from a wholesaler and fill your orders.

Shirt Factory. Design and print art on sweatshirts, T-shirts, polo shirts, and bandannas for school clubs and sports teams. Also look for customers among community organizations and sports leagues.

Just My Type. Type reports for high school and college students.

Page by Page. If you have access to a computer, offer to create flyers and mailings for small businesses. Lots of people send out Christmas letters; design and print their letters for them.

Part Three

Giving Money

Now that you're making money, it's time to do something with it. The first thing you can do with money is *give it away*. It's a strange concept, and you won't find it in many books on money. But most of those books talk about *your* money. In this book, we're talking about *God's* money. So when we mention the word *giving* we mean *giving it back*. Let's explore this strange, exciting, and world-changing transaction.

Chapter 12
Giving Money to Change the World

Once upon a time, people gave their time and money to help those less fortunate than themselves. They didn't do it out of guilt or because they were told to do so, but because it was the right thing to do. Anything less just wasn't *decent*.

Nowadays, things are different. For most of us, providing for the needy isn't our problem anymore. We figure, "Hey, that's the government's job." And when the government doesn't provide food, shelter, jobs, or medical care, we declare it heartless and unfair. But wait a minute. Isn't *government* just a fancy word for "We the people?"

If the government is heartless and unfair, then it is we who are heartless or unfair. It's not *them*, it's *us*. In that case, how can "the government" be more caring and giving than we are?

It can't. We're it. *We the people* are either caring or uncaring. Giving or selfish. Filled with generous compassion, or driven by cold, heartless greed. It's up to us to decide who we are.

And since "we" is just a giant collection of individuals, each person must decide that issue personally—"Who am I? Am I compassionate? Am I willing to sacrifice what I've earned to help others?"

Way too many people answer these questions by saying, "I pay my taxes, and a portion of those taxes goes to help others. That's how I handle my compassionate giving." And that's a lousy answer. If your only giving is in the form of taxes, you're missing out on a thrilling and powerful way to give.

WHAT HAPPENS WHEN YOU GIVE ON YOUR OWN

Taxes are important, and compulsory. Giving on your own is not only voluntary, but filled with great benefits.

YOU HELP THE PEOLE YOU WANT

Congress decides where your tax dollars go. So the money often goes to the agencies with the right political connections or the most media coverage. By giving on your own, you ensure the survival and growth of private agencies that don't get government funds and those without headline-grabbing missions.

IT'S FUN

If you like Christmas because you enjoy watching your family open gifts you've made or bought for them, then why wait all year to feel that thrill? Giving a portion of your income each month spreads the Christmas spirit all over the calendar.

YOU FEEL SIGNIFICANT

There are several billion people on this planet. But something inside you is driving you to be more than a number in the world census. You want your life to count for something. For lots of things. If you give $24 each month to sponsor a child in another country, you're paying for his food, clothing, and education. You may not know the square root of 225 or how to spell Albuquerque (or is it Albakurkey?), and you may not be able to do five pull-ups or empty the trash without being reminded; but you're risking your money to keep someone else *alive*—and that's at least a trillion times more impressive than good spelling.

YOU SET PEOPLE FREE

When you give to organizations that help the needy, you're giving others the opportunity to experience the freedom you enjoy. Most people in this world are trapped by something they can't get out of—hunger, disease, thirst, poverty, war, handicap, or spiritual darkness. People *want* to taste freedom. Your giving makes that possible.

APPEARANCE OF GUILT

I give for all the above reasons. And I'll admit to another—I feel guilty. I don't have to look very far to feel that guilt. I can get there just by looking in the mirror. Here's what I'm wearing:

Reebok shoes	$ 70
socks	$ 5
Levi 501s	$ 35
Superman underwear	$ 5
cotton shirt	$ 25
jacket	$ 75
Casio watch	$ 65
leather wallet	$ 20
TOTAL	$300

The average person in Haiti makes $300 per year. Right now I'm *wearing* what the average Haitian earns in a year. Something inside me declares foul. It's not my mind. My mind is saying, "The cost of living is lower in Haiti, so $300 goes much further there." My mind also points out to me, "You dress like a slob—you don't *deserve* to feel guilty until you've got some jewelry, designer labels, and a Rolex watch."

But my heart still tells me that, despite all logic, there's something wrong with my *always wanting more* without considering those who have less. So I give, and it makes me appreciate the incredible riches I have and think less about the silly things I don't have hanging in my closet.

In 1995, the average American churchgoer gave less than 2.5% of disposable income to a church.

GIVING
SOMETHING BACK

Any of the above reasons is reason enough for any teenager to give. As a Christian, you have the best reason of all. When you give, you're just giving God's money back to God.

If you believe that God is the ultimate provider of things, then giving to others is one of the ways you can thank him for the opportunity to use his money to meet your own needs and desires. Many Christians take a tenth of what they have and use it to give thanks for the nine-tenths they have the privilege of using. Other people give more than that—some giving nearly everything they have. (This percentage-giving is also called *tithing,* from an Old English word meaning "tenth.") For a Christian, giving is one of the most thrilling acts of faith we can experience.

Giving is a thrill. It's thrilling for the giver, for the recipient, and, I'm guessing, is pretty fun for God too. If you already give a portion of your income, you know what I'm talking about. If you don't . . . well, what can I say? You're missing out. Whatever you buy with that money can never do as much for you and the rest of the world as the simple act of giving it away.

In the next chapter I'll show you a plan for giving. It fits in your budget, it's easy to manage, and best of all, it rocks the world. I dare you to read it and to do what it says. But if you do, hold on tight, because your life will never be the same.

Chapter 13

How to Give Away Your Money Like a Maniac

Lots of people give money every once in a while—usually when someone asks for it. But the real power in giving comes when you give every month to the same causes. The best kind of giving adds up, little by little, month to month, year to year, like a savings account. But with giving, you're saving more than money. If you'd like to give a portion of your income regularly, here are some steps to help you get started.

GETTING STARTED

1. PICK A PERCENTAGE

Choose a percentage of your income that you'd like to give each month. Work with that bonehead-easy budget I showed you to make sure that you can afford the amount you commit to.

Keep track of all INCOME so you'll know how much to base your percentage on.

2. PICK A DAY

Decide which day of the month you plan to do your giving. Mark it in your calendar. Treat that day like a celebration—a festive ceremony in which you give back to God a portion he's given to you.

3. DECIDE WHOM YOU WANT TO GIVE TO

Keep your eyes open, ask around. Needs aren't hard to find. Do some homework to make sure the organizations are legitimate—doing what they say they're doing with your money. *And pray about it!* After all, it's God's money, and he has something to say about where you send it.

4. COMMIT TO GIVING A CERTAIN AMOUNT EACH MONTH FOR ONE YEAR

Take an average of your last few months' income and multiply this by your giving percentage—that's how much you can commit every month. For example, if you make about $250 a month and you're planning to give 10%, you'll have about $25 in your GIVING account each month. Now divide that amount among those you plan to give to.

It's smart to leave yourself a little pad in case you bring in less money some months. This leftover amount will show up as the growing balance on your GIVING ledger. If your income drops one month, you can use this balance to cover your giving commitment. If that balance grows and grows you can increase the amount you give to each recipient, or add a new recipient to your list.

5. TEAM UP

Don't be afraid to team up with friends to give your giving greater impact. For example, you may not be able to afford giving $24 a month to sponsor a needy child, but if you find a friend who wants to join you, each can contribute $12 per month. If that's too steep, find three other friends so that each of you can contribute $6. Teaming up enables you to maximize your giving.

GRADUATING

If you follow the above steps, you'll take part in a successful, thrilling adventure in giving. Each month, you'll say thanks to God, change the lives of others, and know a personal satisfaction that I cannot describe in words. But wait.

It gets *better*. Because soon it will be time to *graduate*. Each year, add a point to your giving percentage. If you give 10% this year, then graduate to 11% next year. You'll hardly notice the increase—especially when you

"They all gave out of their wealth; but she, out of her poverty, put in everything."—Jesus

get a raise in your allowance or hourly wage—but it will make a *big* difference in your giving over time.

Imagine this: you're 16, and you decide to give 10% of your income this year, adding a percent each year. Let's assume that you earn about $200 a month, and you get raises every year.

Weekly Budget				
Age	Monthly Income	Annual Income	Giving Percentage	Annual Giving
16	$200	$2,400	10%	$240
17	$250	$3,000	11%	$330
18	$300	$3,600	12%	$432
19	$350	$4,200	13%	$546
20	$400	$4,800	14%	$672
			Total Giving in 5 Years: $2,220	

If you're really bold, you won't wait till the new year to graduate. Instead, give your giving a raise every time you get a raise in your wage. You could be giving 20% in a few years. And if you're an absolute maniac, you'll *start* your giving at 15% or even 20% and graduate from there.

Things get totally crazy when you start working a full-time job. Imagine giving 15% of your $20,000 annual salary. That's $3,000 in just one year. Your GIVE account would have a major impact on your world.

Give to your church to help pay for the youth ministry:	$1,500
Provide food, education, and medical care for two needy kids:	$ 576
Support a missionary overseas for $30 a month:	$ 360
Support a shelter for homeless women:	$ 400
Give money to a family who lost their house in a flood:	$ 164
Total Giving in One Year:	$3,000

What could you possibly buy that would deliver this much happiness? Nothing. That's the cool thing about giving money back to God. He always knows the *perfect* gifts to give. He takes back the money he's given you, and he does stuff with it that you couldn't even dream. He was the instigator of that first Christmas, and he's been giving the world great stuff ever since. Give him a regular and growing portion of your income, and he'll turn it into gifts that will rock the world. Start now with whatever you're earning—no matter how small. And when the big bucks start pouring in, you'll see him change the world in even bigger ways. He promises as much:

> *"Well done, good and faithful servant! You have been faithful with a few things; I will put you in charge of many things. Come and share your master's happiness!"*
> —Matthew 25:21

123

Saving Money

There are three things you can do with the money you make: GIVE it, SAVE it, and SPEND it. We covered that great giving thing. Now let's talk about another great financial pastime: saving. In this next part, I'll show you how bank accounts and other types of investments work, teach  you a few simple investment tricks, and then show you how to save up big stacks of cash quickly. Your future is riding on this stuff, so let's get to it.

Chapter 17

Investment Tricks
No One Will Tell You

I'm about to tell you some stuff that a lot of people don't want you to know. You see, youth marketers are growing filthy rich off your hard-earned cash, and what I'm going to tell you will foil their schemes. That's because the three investment tricks you're about to learn will show you how to invest more of your money into *your* future, not theirs. If you follow my advice, you won't be putting any of them out of business. But if a *bunch* of readers like you try these tricks, a few of them might have to drive BMWs instead of Lambourghinis. What a shame.

Here's another shame. These tricks are so simple, you'd think that more people would try them. But most people don't. Instead, they squander all their cash on stupid purchases, then complain that the rich keep getting richer, while *they* just keep getting poorer. It doesn't take an economics degree to figure out that those marketers keep getting richer off *their* money—money that they practically throw at them.

Well, some people are just going to be stupid with their money, and there's really nothing we can do to stop them.

But I'm figuring that you're not like that. If you've made it this far in the book, you're smart enough to see that you can pull off these investment tricks.

1. INVEST IN THINGS THAT GO UP IN VALUE

Think of it this way; every dollar you spend is an *investment.* What you buy with that buck can do one of two things: it can go up in value, or it can go down in value. The moment you buy a stereo, music album, pair of shoes, or sunglasses, you start losing money because you can never sell that used item for the price you paid when it was new. That's called *depreciation.* That's bad.

Wait. It gets worse. When an item depreciates, you not only lose money in the value of the thing, you also lose the money you *would have gained* had you invested instead in something that goes up in value. That's called *opportunity cost.* Let me show you what these things look like.

Let's say you and your friend Sigfried each had $500 in cash and went shopping for new stereos. He decided to buy a turbo-charged model that's so powerful the lights dim when you switch it on. He blew his entire $500 savings on this thing. A year later, he decided to go on a ski trip, raising the cash by selling his used stereo to

127

someone's kid brother for $300. Sigfried's *cost* of very loud music for the year comes to $200.

But you decided you could survive on your clock radio—and listening to Sigfried's stereo from a block away. So instead of spending $500 on a new stereo, you invested your $500 at the bank in a one-year *certificate of deposit* (CD) account that yields about 5% interest. At the end of the year you had $500 in *principal* and about $25 in *interest*. Now pay attention, because this next part is tricky. Sigfried lost out on this $25 opportunity—he couldn't earn that interest on his $500 because he spent the money on the stereo. That's his *opportunity cost*. The $25 opportunity cost plus the $200 depreciation actually made him $240 poorer than you at the end of the year. Bummer for him. And it gets worse.

Let's say he decided against that ski trip and kept the stereo for five years. (Now his neighbors are bummed.) In five years his $500 stereo investment is worthless—no one wants to buy an old, broken-down stereo. But you, wise one, kept reinvesting in one-year CDs yielding 5%. Your investment is now worth about $638.

I admit it. There's nothing wrong with buying a stereo. I have one myself. But before you purchase a stereo, car, shoes, or just about any consumer item, take a moment to consider the *true* price. If you sell it, you can't get as much as you paid for it. When it goes down in value, you *lose* money. That's *depreciation*.

What's more, each time you invest in something that depreciates, you also lose the opportunity to earn interest

---

Investing Up
$500 investment after 5 years

	cool stereo	CD account
original investment:	$500	$500
interest income:	+$ 0	+$138
depreciation:	−$500	−$ 0
opportunity cost:	−$138	−$ 0
Total Profit/Loss:	−$638	+$138
5-Year Yield:	−128%	+28%

---

on that money. That's *opportunity cost*. The dozens of little things you spend money for each month may not seem to make much of a difference in your future. But they add up to lots of cash—cash that could be *earning* money instead. Right now, when you don't have to pay for rent, home insurance, grocery bills, and medical expenses, you can be saving a larger percentage of your income. If you really want to save money, avoid spending it on things that go down in value.

In other words, invest in things that go *up*. Let's move on.

2. NEVER BORROW MONEY TO BUY THINGS THAT GO DOWN IN VALUE

Let's welcome your friend Winona to the story. When Winona saw Sigfried's stereo, she fell in love . . . with the stereo, not Sigfried, sadly. She rushed out the next day and bought the same screaming model. But Winona had only $50 to spend, so she used it as a *down payment*. The store eagerly arranged to lend her $450 at 18% interest, which she could pay back in 12 monthly payments of $41.25. Now brace yourself, because Winona is losing money in *three* exciting ways:

Depreciation: Her stereo is losing value. Duh.

Opportunity cost: Her money could be *earning* interest instead.

Finance charge: She's paying *interest* on the loan.

Because of the finance charge, Winona wastes more money that could have been earning interest, so her opportunity cost is even higher than Sigfried's.* At the end of five years Winona's stereo is worthless. When you

---

* Let's assume that she could have put the initial $50 in a savings account paying 4% interest compounded daily, and added $41.25 per month to the account. At the end of the year, she would have $556 in her savings account, which she could put in a 5% yielding CD account for the next four years. Some restrictions apply. Rates subject to change. Substantial penalty for early withdrawal. See your local banker. An equal opportunity lender. Member, FDIC. Don't you wish you had ignored this footnote?

The Cost of Borrowing $500 investment after 5 years		
	cool stereo	CD account
original investment:	$500	$500
interest income:	+$ 0	+$138
depreciation:	−$500	−$ 0
opportunity cost:	−$176	−$ 0
finance charge:	−$ 45	−$ 0
Total Profit/Loss:	−$721	+$138
5-Year Yield:	−144%	+28%

figure in the depreciation, opportunity cost, and finance charges, she "paid" $721 for that cool stereo sound. Right about now she's wishing she had fallen in love with Sigfried instead of his stereo. Remember, you *made* $138—and you've still got the original $500.

If you're trying to save money for a car, an education—*anything*—then don't borrow money for something that depreciates in value. While the bank is paying you 4% to 6% or more in interest in your savings account, you're paying the bank—or some other lender—15% to 20% interest for the right to *borrow it back*. Does this sound ridiculous to you? It should! It's like trying to go up the down escalator.

But as I said before, most people don't follow this advice. They buy on credit and lose in interest charges some or all of the gain in their appreciating investments. It's the American way. And it's just plain stupid. Don't be that way. You're smarter than that. Don't borrow money to pay for things that go down in value. For more on the thrills and chills of borrowing, see chapter 22, "How to Borrow Money (But Don't)." But not right now. We're getting to the good part.

3. Make an Appreciating Investment with Every Paycheck

Maybe you're planning to start investing as soon as you have "enough." You know, when you get a *real* job . . . when you start working more hours . . . when the *big* paychecks start rolling in. *Then* you'll have a fat chunk of money that's worth saving. But let's look at this plan realistically. Unless you win the lottery or rob a bank, you'll never suddenly have one big chunk to invest. When those bigger paychecks start rolling in, so will bigger bills—rent, insurance, grocery bills, *taxes.* Like most of the people who don't follow this simple advice, you'll spend your life waiting for your treasure ship to come in. Hey. I've seen the horizon. That boat's not coming.

Face facts. The only way you'll ever come up with one big stack of cash is to *build it yourself,* one dollar at a time. Here's how: *Make a deposit to your savings account every time you get paid.*

If you receive money every week, your monthly savings account statement should show at least four deposits—and no withdrawals. If you get paid every two weeks, or twice a month, your statement should show deposits for each payday. No excuses.

Here's why. The majority of an adult's income goes to pay for housing, utilities, medical expenses, and the daily costs of living—toothpaste, toilet paper, TV repair, and trash collection. Chances are you don't have any of these expenses. You pay for only a small portion of your food. If you don't pay for a car, gas, or insurance, you have it easy. And if your folks pay for most or all of your clothing, you have it made.

In fact, you may be richer than your parents in terms of *discretionary income*—the money that's left after all the necessary bills are paid. Whether your income is an allowance, a minimum-wage job, baby-sitting money, or a birthday check from your Aunt Elba, you can afford to invest a greater percentage of it than just about any adult on the planet. So do it.

Little by little, paycheck after paycheck, your savings account will grow. You'll earn interest on every penny and attain your big financial dreams *years* sooner than most people. And the discipline you learn from this simple habit will pay big dividends for the rest of your life.

Okay, let's review these three simple investment tricks before some rich marketer makes us forget them:

> 1. *Invest in things that go up.* (And don't waste money on things that go the other way.)

In 1929, the U.S. shrunk the size of its paper money by 31%.

2. *Never borrow money to buy things that go down in value.* (You'll lose money in three costly ways.)

3. *Make an appreciating investment with every paycheck.* (Little by little, your savings will grow to something big.)

I *told* you this was simple stuff. Simple to remember. Simple to do. Of course, that pretty much *guarantees* that most people won't even try them. They're waiting for some complicated, sneaky scheme. Let them wait. Be the first on your block to give these tricks a try. Be a rebel.

Chapter 15

How Banks Work

The first and totally obvious way to save up your money is to put it in the bank. Duh. You know that. But you may not know exactly how banks work, the various accounts they offer, and why it's important to shop around for your banking needs. That's what this chapter is all about.

Banks and savings and loans are good at coming up with fancy names for their accounts; names like "Advantage Plus Mega-Money Super Savings Certificate Account." But most of their accounts fit into one of four basic categories:

1. *Basic savings* accounts (sometimes called passbook accounts) have little or no minimum balance and pay minimum interest. *Advantages:* You can withdraw your money whenever you want (no minimum deposit period), and you earn more interest than if you hid the money in that secret place near your bed

The average life of a $1 bill is 13 to 18 months.

(shh!). *Disadvantage:* You don't earn much interest.

2. *Basic checking* accounts don't pay interest, but they don't cost you anything as long as you keep a minimum balance, typically $500 to $800. If your balance drops below the minimum, the bank will charge you a monthly fee of $5 to $10. Some banks also charge you a few cents per check, or tack on a fee each time you use an ATM.

3. *Money market* checking and savings accounts pay better interest than basic savings accounts, with the rate rising according to the amount of the balance. They also have higher minimum balances, usually $1,000 or more.

4. *Certificates of deposit* (CDs) are guarantees that you will let the bank keep a certain amount of money (generally $1,000 or more) for a certain period (typically, one month to 10 years) in exchange for higher interest. If you need your money before the CD matures, you will pay a stiff penalty. Obviously, the more money you give them and the longer they keep it, the more interest they'll guarantee. Some banks offer $500 CDs, which makes them a good investment possibility for lots of teenagers.

JUGGLING INTEREST

Before you go shopping for a bank investment, you'll need to know how banks figure interest. There are two kinds: the kind you *pay,* and the kind you *receive.* Here's how it works when you're on the receiving end.

Let's say that while walking out of a store, you hold the door for a man who's entering. He's amazed at your politeness and hands you $10,000 as a gesture of his thanks. When the crowd revives you from fainting, you remember the $10,000 in your pocket and race to the bank. You deposit the money into an account at a 6% annual percentage rate (APR), *compounded monthly.* The "6%" part sounds good; the "compounded" part sounds like something for warts. But you make your deposit and go off to tell your friends what happened. The bank puts your money into a little envelope with your name on it and hides it in their vault.

On the first day of the next month, a little man named Harold takes his calculator into the vault to count the money in your envelope: $10,000 (phew!)— which he multiplies by ½ of 1% (.005). Your question at this point should be, "Why the heck did Harold pick *that* number?"

It's ½₂ of 6%—one month's worth of your interest rate. When he multiplies your $10,000 by .005, his calculator will show that the bank owes you $50 in interest for the first month. Then he takes $50 out of a little green money bag he carries and places it in your envelope.

The next month Harold is at it again. He counts the money in your envelope—$10,050, multiplies it by .005, then puts $50.25 into your envelope. Harold does this every month for the year. "Compounded monthly" means Harold takes his calculator into the vault once a month. (Actually, one time he was sick so Hector did it.)

At the end of the year, you decide to withdraw your money. Out of the vault comes your envelope: your original $10,000 plus $616.78 in interest. Wait a minute: 6% of $10,000 is $600—you were overpaid $16.78. Not really. The extra amount was the interest you received on the *interest*. That's what's called *compounded* interest.

Figuring the Yield	
(6% interest compounded monthly)	
interest after 1 year:	$616.78
original investment:	$10,000
Annual Yield:	6.17%

In money talk, your *principal* of $10,000 *yielded* 6.17% interest. *Yield* is a useful word that money people borrowed from farmers. It simply refers to the produce you harvest after planting something. In this case, you planted ten grand in the bank, and a year later your money crop produced 6.17% more than you started with.

Let's say you decide to put your money in an account paying the same 6% interest, but this time it's

compounded *yearly*. Twelve months after you deposit the money, Harold takes his calculator into the vault to figure your interest: $10,000 x .06 (12 months' worth of interest) = $600. Your yield on this account: 6%. This is not only a worse deal for you, but really boring for Harold.

Comparing Yields
($10,000 invested for 1 year at 6%)

compounding	interest	yield
yearly:	$600.00	6.00%
monthly:	$616.78	6.17%
daily:	$618.31	6.18%

The way to compare interest accounts is by their *yields*—what you get out of them. As you can see, the shorter the compounding period, the more money you make in interest.

Before we go on, I feel obligated to tell you the truth: Harold doesn't go into the vault to count your money. Two reasons. First, there's no one named Harold at your bank—several years ago he was replaced by a computer (I know . . . it's sad) that automatically calculates your interest at each compounding.

Second, your money isn't in the vault. The bank loaned it to a woman named Rita who is planning to open the Reptile Emporium down the street (really). Rita is paying the bank 10% interest for the $10,000.

After paying your interest, the bank still makes 4% on the deal.*

Which brings up the *other* type of interest: the kind you pay. With a loan, the interest is the fee you pay for the privilege of using the lender's money. Let's say the reptile lady's loan must be paid back all at once at the end of a year. At that time, she gives the bank the principal (the original $10,000) plus 10%, or $1,000 in *simple* interest. In other words, the interest is calculated *once*—there's no compounding as in a savings account. Most lenders charge simple interest. However, there are certain exceptions, and they can get nasty. (See chapter 22.)

MAKING MONEY AT THE BANK

Bank CDs (Certificates of Deposit) are a smart investment for teenagers. Unlike most other investments, gains are guaranteed, and the interest rate is higher than a regular savings account. And because your money is locked up for the prescribed time period, you can't spend it on a new wardrobe in a fit of insanity. If you have money sitting in a savings account or piggy bank, stick it in a CD and start earning some real interest.

But there's just one problem. What if you don't have the $500 or $1,000 minimum to open a CD? Three solutions:

---

* OK, OK . . . there's more to it than this, such as the length of the reptilean loan, whether it's being paid off monthly or all at once, and so on. But this is just an illustration—can we go on?

1. *Sweating.* Save your allowance, store up the birthday checks, work a few extra hours—and above all, *spend less.*

2. *Pooling.* You're not the only one with this problem. Find one or two friends with some money to invest. Put in identical amounts and set up the account so that each of you has to sign for the money. At the end of the period divide the principal and interest evenly.

3. *Bumping.* Hang out in front of the bank. If a rich old lady walks out carrying a handful of cash, accidentally bump into her and see if she drops it. Just kidding—bumping is like pooling, except you're just using someone else's money to bump you into the "big leagues." A relative with money in the bank may be willing to let you use a few hundred dollars of it for a bump if you agree to pay her the portion of the interest that's hers. For example, if she puts in $700 to bump your $300, pay her 70% of the yield. Keep track of her money, and repay it when your savings can stand on its own.

If you're investing in CDs, it's best to track the direction of interest rates each week or so. Big banks sometimes record their latest interest rates on an 800 number you can call. If your bank doesn't do this, just call the local branch and ask. You can also check for a sign or flyer inside the bank whenever you drop by to make one of your regular deposits.

If interest rates are on the rise, invest in CDs with terms of one to six months: the faster the rise, the shorter the term. The reason is you don't want to lock your money up at a lower rate when you could be getting better interest soon. The opposite is also true: if interest rates are falling (and you think they'll continue to do so), lock in a high rate for a year or two. It's also good to compare your bank's CD rate with rates at other banks in your area just to make sure they're paying you a competitive rate. If not, consider opening an account at the bank with the higher rate.

When a CD matures (i.e., the time period is up), you've got to decide what to do with the money: invest in another CD, deposit the money in a savings account, or take it out of the bank. Make your decision before the CD matures so the money doesn't sit around, earning little or no interest while you make up your mind. Some banks will automatically "roll over" the money for you by investing it in another CD. Others may stick it in a money market account till you make up your mind. But don't wait for them to do something—mark the maturity date in your calendar, and make your move the day it matures.

BANKING ON YOUR FUTURE

Later, I'll show you how to achieve specific savings goals. But whatever those goals, you'll need some bank accounts to reach them. Here's what you'll need:

1. *A checking account.* If you don't have a checkbook, get one. Some banks may require you to have an adult named on the account; others will open an account for minors without an adult. As we discussed in chapter 5, "Get a Checking Account," the checking account acts like your INCOME envelope. All your income goes into that account, then gets distributed among your other priorities. Remember that your checking account is just a "holding tank"—the money in it is destined for other priorities such as giving, saving, and spending.

2. *A savings account.* If you don't already have one, open a savings account now. Then use it! Each time you get paid, deposit a portion of your income in your savings account. Each month, your savings account statement should show at least four deposits and no withdrawals. It doesn't matter if your deposits are small. Your budget should contain a percentage figure for savings. Your account statement is proof that you are serious about that budget.

Together, these two accounts will help you manage your money and put away more of it in savings to fund your future.

Washington must have thrown a Spanish peso across the Potomac (the U.S. didn't mint silver dollars until 1792).

Chapter 16
Mutual Funds Explained Pretty Clearly

So far we've talked about using savings accounts and CDs to save up stacks of cash. There are lots of other investments out there—stocks, bonds, precious metals, commodities, and many more. Most of these kinds of investments don't really work for teenagers because they require large amounts of money to get started. There are some exceptions, but I'll save those for the next chapter.

There's one nonbank investment that works just fine for teenagers—mutual funds. They don't require lots of money to get started, and they can make your savings grow faster than a bank account. Here's how they work.

Let's say you have $500 to invest in something. You could buy 100 shares of a stock trading at $5 per share, but that's putting all your eggs in one basket. If the stock does poorly, you'll lose some or all of your investment. Not a good idea.

Better to spread your money around. One way to spread your investment is to buy shares of stock in several companies, but I'll be honest here; in the stock world, $500 is not a lot to work with. If you spent it buying $100 worth of stock in five companies, the stockbroker might charge you $200 or more just to handle the transactions. Your investment will have to yield over 40% just to break even. Fat chance. And too expensive.

Here's another way: Find nine friends who each have $500 to invest. Put all your money together to create a $5000 *fund*. Now you can buy several stocks with this fund and spread the risks and costs between you. The stockbroker's fees are less because you're buying more shares of each stock. Your share in this fund is 10% of every stock owned by the group. If one company doesn't do well, the performance of the others can offset the loss.

The problem with that plan is that it's hard to find nine friends with that much money to invest. And even if you find them, trying to agree on which investments to make can wipe out a bunch of friendships in a hurry. Fortunately, you don't have to form an investment fund with your friends. Many investors have already formed funds just like this one, but bigger. They're called *mutual funds*.

A BIG CLUB FOR YOUR MONEY

With a mutual fund, *thousands* of people invest varying amounts, and professional managers choose which investments will be best for everyone in the group. Since the fund manager often has millions and millions of dollars to work with, he or she can spread the money around, investing in 50 to 100 different *securities* (stocks, bonds, etc.).

In other words, your $500 (or whatever amount you invest) is pooled with millions of dollars and invested by professionals who follow the financial markets daily.

Mutual funds are a popular idea. There are hundreds to choose from, each with specific investment goals to appeal to certain kinds of investors. Here are the most popular types of mutual funds:

- *Growth funds* invest your money in securities (stocks, bonds, etc.) that will (hopefully) increase in value. *Aggressive growth funds* invest in new and growing industries and companies with risky but potentially big-time futures. *Moderate growth* funds take their chances with more established, growing companies. If these companies do well, the value of their stocks rise, and so does the value of your mutual fund shares. If they do poorly, the value goes down.

- *Equity income funds* invest in stocks that pay regular dividends. You receive a quarterly check of your share of all the dividends paid to the fund. If you prefer, you can arrange to have your dividends reinvested (i.e., used to buy more shares in the fund).

- *Growth and income funds* invest in both kinds of securities. If the fund manager is successful, the value of your shares goes up, *and* you get some dividend money each quarter.

- *Money market funds* invest in bank CDs (certificates of deposit), Treasury bills (short-term loans to the government), and other short-term loans to corporations and municipalities (local governments).

- *Bond funds* invest in bonds, which pay steady interest.

Some mutual funds focus on a specific portion of the economy as a way to achieve their goals. *Tax-free funds* invest in government bonds; the government makes investing in these lower-yield bonds enticing by allowing you to exclude the dividends from your taxable income. Most teenagers don't have tax bills large enough to justify this type of investment.

Other funds invest in a particular industry, region, or country: a *sector fund* may invest only in high-technology companies, or agricultural firms, or those in the aerospace business. *International funds* invest in specific foreign regions or countries, such as companies based in Asia or those doing business in Mexico. *Precious metal funds* invest in companies that mine and sell gold, silver, or platinum.

In 1990, New Zealand stopped the use of their 1 cent and 2 cent coins.

FUNDS FOR TEENAGERS

As a general rule, *growth funds* are best for teenagers. They're riskier than most of the others, but they have the potential to make you more money. An aggressive growth fund could yield 30 to 40% in one year—or *lose* that much or more. There are plenty of less radical mutual funds that still tend to do much better than your bank account.

Unless you need every dime of your money to spend for college next year, you can probably afford to take moderate risks with your money. No one wants to lose money, but as long as you don't take stupid risks, you probably won't lose more money than you can replace quickly with a part-time job. Invest no more than half of your savings in a solid mutual fund. If the fund is risky (potential for big losses), don't put in more than a fourth of your savings.

An income or money market fund will pay you regular dividends, but you don't need the income right now—you'd just have to reinvest the money anyway. Tax-free funds are reliable, but they usually yield less than other funds. You don't need the safety as much as an adult does, and your tax bill isn't high enough to make the tax benefits pay off.

How to Invest

Most mutual funds are sold directly by the investment companies and financial institutions that manage them. But before accepting your money, a fund is required to send you a *prospectus*—a report describing the fund's investment goals, risks, trading procedures, and past performance. After doing your research and reading the prospectus, if you do decide to buy shares in a fund, you'll have to send a check for at least the minimum amount, typically $250 to $1,000. After that, you can usually make additional investments of $250 or more, as often as you like.

Here's a catch. You need to be 18 to invest in a mutual fund by yourself. If you're not, you can ask an adult to buy the shares for you as a "gift," under the Uniform Gift to Minors Act (UGMA). The investment is yours, but your *trustee* (the adult) is legally responsible for the transactions. The fund office will tell you how to do this.

Like many legal documents, prospectuses are not always easy to understand. A good source of mutual fund information is *Money* magazine, which tracks the best performing funds each month in a variety of categories. They also tell you how various funds have done over the past year and five years. Their listings also include toll-free numbers you can call to receive prospectuses. Annually, *Money, Business Week,* and other magazines print ratings for all major mutual funds to help you compare funds and learn about their managers' strategies.

In 1273, Kubla Khan issued paper money made from mulberry bark.

FUNDING YOUR FUTURE

Mutual funds are a great way to set aside chunks of cash to fund your future dreams. Pick the right ones, and your money will be safe from those disasterous spending impulses we all get when we see something shiny in a store window. And while the money is locked up, it grows. At least that's what it *should* do. Remember, with a mutual fund there's no guarantee.

Later in this section of the book, I'll show you how to invest just a portion of your savings in a mutual fund, which limits the risks and maximizes its potential for growth.

Chapter 17
Other Investments

As you can tell, I think mutual funds are a wise investment for teenagers. They spread your risk among many companies, and let you take advantage of the wisdom of people who know a lot about investing. Then there are all those other investments, but they're not practical for most teenagers.

That's because most investments are designed for adults with lots of money to play with. And even if you have lots of cash to invest, your investment goals are different from the average adult's. For example, you have a lower income, but a larger percentage of your income can be used for investing. And you're not worried about retirement right now—you're too busy raising money for a car or college tuition.

In short, you're different. That means you need a different approach to investing. A different strategy.

TEENAGE INVESTMENT STRATEGY

I don't know your financial situation or what you dream of doing in your future. But if you're like most teenagers, you have a specific high-dollar dream in your immediate future, whether it's a car, a college education, or even a three-month overseas mission trip after you graduate from high school. Whatever your next big financial goal, this four-step strategy can help you reach it.

1. GO FOR GROWTH

Your number one investment goal is to make your money *grow*. Right now you have few expenses compared to your income. But soon you'll be paying for cars, education, furniture, entertainment, clothes, food, housing, medical expenses, and a thousand other things that someday will obliterate your paycheck. Make the right investments now, and your money will grow substantially until you *really* need it.

Look for investments that will make your money grow. Money hidden under your mattress or buried in a shoe box in your backyard is *not* growing. Interest earned in a savings account or CD must be reinvested immediately. That leads to the second point.

2. DON'T BOTHER WITH INCOME INVESTMENTS

Some people rely upon dividends and interest to help pay their regular living expenses. Retired people count on their income investments to take the place of those regular paychecks they no longer receive. People who need a steady income from their investments put their money in bonds, high-yield stocks, and mutual funds based on these investments to ensure that they'll get regular checks in the mail.

But you don't have very many living expenses, and the ones you have can easily be covered with a part-time job or even your allowance. Invest in things that go up in value. Most bonds, many stocks, and "income" mutual funds pay regular interest or dividends. You don't need that income. You need *growth*. If you have investments that pay interest or dividends, reinvest these "bonuses" immediately, and keep your money growing.

3. TAKE SOME RISKS

Mutual funds that grow quickly are risky investments. But more than just about any other age group, you can probably afford to take those risks. Your salary will only increase as you get older, and you can replenish what you lose much faster because you can put into savings the money that adults have to put into housing, food, medical costs, and other living expenses. At the same time, you want to keep at least ½ of your savings in insured, guaranteed investments such as bank CDs and money market accounts. If the money is your ticket to college, limit your risky investments to ⅓ or ¼ of your savings.

4. LARGE CASH RESERVES AREN'T CRITICAL

Most adults try to keep a large reserve in a savings account in case they have a major emergency or are out of work for a few months. It's different with you: If you lose your job, you probably won't be evicted from your home. In fact, for you, the opposite strategy is best. If your money is locked up in investments that can't be cashed in quickly, you won't be tempted to squander it on less important things now.

Of course, as you get older, your financial situation will change, and so will your investment plan. But right now, you're saving for something big and soon—a car, college tuition, whatever. If that's your case, the above strategy will help you maximize the growth of your savings.

Now you can see why bank accounts and mutual funds are the way to go. If your goals are further into the future, or you have great gobs of cash to invest, you can look into other investment opportunities. Here's a very brief explanation of the two most popular investment types: stocks and bonds.

STOCKS

When you own a share of stock, you own a portion of the company. If the company does well and the stock value goes up, you can sell your share for a *capital gain.* If the company has healthy profits, it may set aside a portion to send to each shareholder in the form of a *dividend.* Those are the two main ways of making money with stock.

To buy stock you have to use a middleman called a *stockbroker,* who charges you a commission for his work. With a "full service" broker, the minimum commission (for the smallest orders) is about $40. If you buy $500 worth of stock in one company, you'll have to earn 8% on the investment just to cover the commission. When you sell it, you'll pay another $40. That means that your stock has to rise in value by 16% or pay huge dividends just for you to break even.

Some brokers charge less, including many that do business on the Internet. But any broker will charge you a fee for transacting your trades, so you must figure these costs into your plans. As a rule, small investments in stock are expensive. Stock mutual funds are a better deal for smaller investors.

BONDS

Bonds are loans to companies and governments. With most bonds, you lend the issuer $1,000 for a certain time period—up to 30 years. They send you the interest every year and give you the $1,000 back at the end of the loan. Bonds are good for people who need to earn a regular income from their investments to cover expenses. But you already have income from an allowance or part-time job, so you're better off with investments that grow bigger, such as growth funds and CDs.

There are two types of bonds that don't spread your interest out over time: *U.S. Savings Bonds* are loans to the government. When the term is up (typically five years or more), you can cash in the bond to get back your original investment plus interest. These bonds don't pay high interest, but they're guaranteed and a good way to lock your money away so you won't spend it.

Zero-coupon bonds also grow bigger over time. Instead of paying you the interest each year ("coupons," in the bond world), they pay it all at once at the end of the loan. With U.S. Savings Bonds and zero-coupon bonds, you have to make sure that the term expires in time for your college needs, or whatever you plan to do with the money. There's no sense in stowing away big amounts of cash in bonds if you can't get to it when you need it most.

AND MORE

If you're interested in learning more about stocks, bonds, and other types of investments, check your library for books that cover these topics in depth. Here's one book I recommend: *The Wall Street Journal Guide to Money and*

Markets. It does an excellent job of explaining stuff in simple terms. And best of all, it has plenty of pictures, so even I can understand it.

For now, you've got a good basic understanding of how banks and mutual funds work, and an investment strategy that works for teenagers. Now let's get down to dollars and cents, how to save up a big stack of cash. That sounds like a good chapter title. Let's use it. Please continue.

In the 1870s you could be fined $10 for throwing a paper dart in the New York Stock Exchange.

Chapter 18
How to Save up a Big Stack of Cash

Chances are, you've got your heart set on a big purchase in your future; a car, a college education, a beach house in Tahiti (we can dream). Whatever your plans, saving up a big stack of cash is essential to them. What will it take to reach your financial goals? How can you set aside *regular, small stacks* of savings cash with every paycheck? I'll show you how to reach your financial goals in the shortest time possible. And *bonus*—you can do it using that bonehead-easy management plan we discussed earlier. It's a foolproof plan (I tested it on myself). Check it out.

GETTING TO YOUR FIRST $500

Here's your first goal: $500. If you're already there, jump to the next goal. If you're not, here's how to get there, whether you have a regular job or not.

If you don't have a regular job, do whatever you can to make at least $15 per week (only $2.14 each day) for a year.

Deposit $10 *every week* into a savings account. If you're making just $15 weekly, this plan will leave you with just five bucks to cover your other priorities. If that's just too far of a stretch, make more money. But don't steal from your savings and giving priorities. Rework your budget—you can figure out a way to make it work.

If you have a regular part-time job, saving $10 a week is easy. In fact, it's *too* easy. Set your sights higher. Increase the weekly savings amount to $15, $20, or $25. Better yet, base your savings figure on a percentage. If your gross paycheck comes to $100 a week, save 25%. When you get a raise, or work more hours, or make extra income from another job, stay at 25%—or increase it to 30%. You'll hardly notice the difference if you're making extra money anyway.

And, of course, don't *borrow* money, and don't make *withdrawals* from your savings account. Now you can see why that budgeting thing is so important. Without it, you'll be stuck without a workable plan to fund your dreams. With it, you'll be on your way to your first $500. And there's more where that came from.

And while you're making those frequent trips to the bank, keep your eye on the interest rates for CD accounts. Many banks post the current rates on a sign inside; if yours doesn't, ask the teller each week. Note which direction the rates are headed: rising? falling? Staying about the same? You'll want to know this fact to make your first new investment. Stay tuned.

GETTING TO $1,000

The day you reach $500, march down to the bank and open a CD account. If your bank requires a higher minimum for this kind of account, call around to find a bank that will accept your $500. Or find a friend or family member who will invest another $500—at the end of the term, you can split the interest you've earned. When you open your CD account, be sure to select the proper term.

If you followed my instructions above, you've been watching the rates each week to see which way they're going. If interest rates are *rising,* choose a *short* term—1 or 3 months if they offer it, but no more than 6 months. You don't want to lock up your money for a year at a lower interest rate if you can get a higher rate a few months from now. Some CDs have variable rates, which means the bank will raise or lower the interest rate if circumstances change. This can be a good thing if interest rates are rising.

Getting to
$1000

Weekly
Savings

CD
$500
(+ interests)

SAVINGS
ACCOUNT

Continue to "roll over" the money in your CD whenever the term is up. Keep your eye on interest rates. If they continue to rise, keep your terms short. It's wise to check other banks' CD rates every few weeks. If someone else is offering a better rate, you can open a new account at the bank with the higher rate as soon as your current account matures.

If interest rates are *falling,* lock in the money for a longer term—1 to 2 years. But be careful—if you're planning to use this money to buy a car or pay for college, make sure the CD will mature in time for your big need. If you withdraw before the end of the term, the penalty you have to pay will wipe out the interest you earned. And there's no point to that.

And while you're juggling your CD, continue your weekly savings plan. Take another look at your budget: Can you squeeze a few more dollars into your savings account each week? Increase your savings percentage by a few points. Another dollar or two will hardly be noticed. If you've been working hard, it may be time for a raise. If you get a 10% raise, give your savings and giving priorities a 10% raise too. They deserve it! For example, if you've been giving 10%, now give 11%. If you've been saving 20%, now save 22%. The increase is a small fraction of a fraction—you'll barely feel it.

Now look at your spending. What buying habits can you reign in? Try one less fast-food meal a week. And one less music CD per month. Postpone buying that new pair of jeans till you know if you *really* want them.

After reworking your budget, set a new savings goal based on your saving and spending changes. If you made your first $500 in 20 weeks, set a goal of 17 weeks to save up the next $500. Every dollar saved will bring you closer to your financial dreams.

You're now on the fast track to $1000. You've got at least $500 earning higher interest in a CD, and you're paying attention to interest rates and terms to squeeze out every penny in interest. And your regular savings account is growing weekly: lots of deposits—with just one withdrawal or transfer to fund your CD account. Before you know it, you'll be staring at a four-figure portfolio.

Time to get ready for your next investment. A mutual fund may be a great investment for you. Start doing your homework now so you'll be ready to invest when you reach your $1000 goal. *Money* magazine prints regular comparisons of mutual fund performances, and newsweeklies, such as *U.S News* publish annual guides. Go to your library, or poke around on the Internet to glean all the information you can. You might also ask your parents, teachers, boss, and friends' parents which mutual funds they might recommend.

GETTING TO $1,500

The first thing you need to do when you reach the $1000 mark is *stop and celebrate!* Congratulations! You've accomplished something great. Treat yourself to a big fat

Getting to
$1500

Weekly
Savings

CD
$500
(+ interests)

Mutual Fund
$500
(+ interests &
dividends)

SAVINGS
ACCOUNT

dessert, or buy a round of french fries for your friends. Chances are, you've been mooching off them for the past few months just to save the money that brought you to this goal. When the party is over, put your four-figure portfolio to work to achieve your next goal: $1,500.

First, make sure your $500 CD is healthy and happy and earning you lots of interest. By this time, it's worth more than $500, because you've been reinvesting that money each time you roll over your account. Depending on interest rates and the length of time it's taken to get here, you may now have $525 or more in that account. Keep it there. It's a safe, sure investment, and no matter what else happens in your investing, you'll always have this steadily growing stack of cash to see you through.

Now it's time to move the brand-new $500 to a more aggressive investment. If you've been doing your home-work on mutual funds, you should have found one that looks good for you. Time to take the plunge. Send in the check, and start watching your money grow. As we discussed, that's not guaranteed. The greater the gains, the greater the risks. But if you choose wisely, you should get a return on your investment that's better than your CD and far better than your regular savings account.

Keep your eye on the fund's performance in the newspaper's financial section or on the Web. If its value falls and keeps falling, you may want to cut your losses, cash in your investment, and invest in a new fund. Don't get jumpy if you see small drops in value—give it some time to prove that it's growing in the long run.

Finally, it's time to rework your budget again. If you've gotten a raise, give your savings and giving priorities a raise too. Rethink your spending priorities. Carry less money in your wallet or purse. Postpone purchasing big-ticket items until you're convinced that you really, really want them. Now set a new savings goal for your next $500. Do what you can to raise it in fewer weeks than last time. If you've gotten this far, you're already becoming an expert at money management. Tweak a few priorities, work a few extra hours, and the next $500 will come quickly.

GETTING TO $2,000

Let's pause a moment and look at how far you've come. You've got that original $500 plus interest, still growing slowly and surely in your CD account. You've got your second $500 invested in a mutual fund—and if you chose wisely, it's growing faster than the CD. The proceeds from the mutual fund (interest and dividends) are being reinvested in the fund, so every dollar is earning its keep.

What's more, you have a brand-new stack of cash piling up in your savings account. Where should you put it? That's up to you. If you'll be needing that money for a car or tuition within the next year, you may want to add it to your CD account or open another CD. Just make sure the CD matures before you'll need your money.

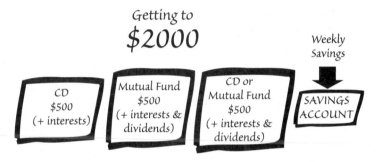

Getting to
$2000

Weekly Savings

| CD $500 (+ interests) | Mutual Fund $500 (+ interests & dividends) | CD or Mutual Fund $500 (+ interests & dividends) | SAVINGS ACCOUNT |

If you won't be needing that money right away and your mutual fund is growing well, you may want to add to your investment there. Or you can try another fund you've been following.

For the next step, you know the routine. Rework your budget, give your savings and giving a raise, and examine your spending habits to make sure you're saving every dollar you can. You'll reach your next goal before you know it.

GETTING TO $2,500 AND BEYOND

By now you're an old pro at this money thing. Just keep managing your existing investments, and transfer your accumulating savings balance to these or new investments as you see fit. If you paid attention, you saw that I followed a few simple guidelines for this strategy.

USE YOUR SAVINGS ACCOUNT AS A STAGING AREA

In other words, use it to store your accumulating weekly contributions until you have a balance large enough to transfer to a higher-yielding investment. If you keep all your savings in a regular savings account, you're missing out on better opportunities.

WORK WITH A SAFETY NET

Your CD account is guaranteed—you can't lose money. It's also insured; if the bank goes out of business, its insurers will cover your investment. In other words, you can't lose. Even if you make risky investments in mutual funds, stocks, or Antarctic real estate and lose every penny, you'll still have that CD to help you get back on your feet.

KEEP A RESERVE

The money accumulating in your savings account is your "reserve supply," just in case something bad happens and you need some cash. For example, if you lose your job you'll have some cash in your savings to cover bills that will still be coming in till you find another job. As your bills grow, so should your reserve. People who live on their own try to keep at least one month's income in their savings as a minimum. Two month's worth is better, and three is ideal. Until you move out on your own, you should be safe with the above plan.

DON'T PUT ALL YOUR EGGS IN ONE BASKET

In money talk, that's called *diversifying your assets*. If all your savings are in a single mutual fund and that fund's value crashes, you'll lose big-time. Spread things out so that a potential loss in one investment can be offset by the success in other investments.

DON'T CASH OUT

The moment you make a withdrawal to spend an investment, you stop getting richer and start getting poorer. When you make a withdrawal or sell an asset, roll the money into another investment—immediately. Every day that it sits in a checking account or your wallet is a day wasted. Keep it working. Unlike the rest of us, money doesn't need a day off. Keep it working seven days a week, every day of the year. That's also true for the interest and dividends you make in your investments. When you're starting out, these bonuses don't seem like much, but when you add them together and keep reinvesting them, they make a big difference over time. Keep every penny on the job, full-time.

NEVER STOP SAVING

It takes real discipline to save up stacks of cash. You've got to save more, spend less, and get better and better at those skills all the time. Once you've mastered these habits, it would be a shame to relapse into your old ways. Habits are much easier to maintain than they are to start. Each time you attain a financial goal, don't treat it as the finish line. Use it as a milestone to celebrate how far you've come. Then set the next goal and continue your journey.

A GLIMPSE AT YOUR FUTURE

The next part of this book is all about how to spend money wisely. But before we go there, I want to wrap up this savings business with a few facts about your future. Here's the first one: *People who don't learn how to save in their teenage years rarely succeed in doing so as adults.*

That's a scary fact. It's so frightening that you'd think more adults would warn you about it. Sadly, they don't. And the adults who do warn you get their message drowned out in the blitzkrieg of advertising pitched at you by every marketer and merchant who's after your cash.

If you take the advertising's advice, you'll abandon your savings goals and spend all your money on piles and piles of *stuff*—stuff that gives momentary pleasure, some laughs, a few thrills, and maybe an occasional jolt of silly pride as you parade it in front of your envious friends. And two or three years from now, you'll have a pile of worthless junk and be no further toward your dreams.

To add insult to injury, you'll have lost this first, best, and only chance to learn how to save. Imagine living the rest of your life unable to attain your dreams. You'll have your heart set on a decent car but settle for a beat-up old thing that breaks down more than it runs. You'll dream of going to college, yet when you discover you can't afford it, you'll wonder if all that junk you bought was really worth more than a good education. And at the risk of sounding like your parents, I'll tell you one more broken dream.

One day you'll want to be married, get a house, raise cool kids, take fun vacations together, make a difference in your world and theirs. But by then you'll be working two jobs, trying to pay off insane credit card debts, spending every dime on loan interest, and kicking yourself because you didn't learn a simple thing like how to save money, back when life was so simple.

I'm sure you've heard plenty of adults like me tell you about the big, scary future. Here's our favorite speech: "The decisions you make today will affect you for the rest of your life." Well, I'll be honest with you, sometimes that's true, and sometimes it's not. I don't know your situation, and I certainly can't predict your future, but I do know this. I've worked with thousands and thousands of teenagers. I've watched hundreds of them grow up. Based upon my observations, I can confidently say that what you decide to do regarding at least these three things will *absolutely* affect you for the rest of your life:

- faith

- sex

- money

The decisions you make today in these three areas will shape your future. The beliefs and habits you form right now will either haunt you or bless you for the rest of your life. No magazine ad or TV commercial will tell you this fact. You won't hear a marketer reveal what your future will *really* look like if you believe everything they say. So I'm telling you instead.

Your future *matters*. God put you on this planet for a *reason*. If you fail to learn how to manage your money now and save for your great big future, you'll be enslaved by money for the rest of your life. God has more important things for you to do.

Get started today. Invest in your future. Take the control of your money away from the marketers and put it back where it belongs—in the future God has planned for you.

By the way, this same advice is true for those other two topics, faith and sex. Take the control of these areas out of the hands of the media, the marketers, and all those who seek to make money at your expense. Let God, not money-hungry grown-ups, be the one who guides your decisions. He's the only one who can truly see your future, the only one who can shape it right.

Part Five

Spending Money

I'm sure that some readers will get to this point in the book and figure I saved the best for last. Actually, I saved the least for last. Of all the things you can do with money, spending it is the least satisfying, least rewarding, and least likely to change your world, now or in the future.

Then again, it's "the best" in certain ways. Spending is the best way to get into debt, the best way to let others take advantage of you, and the best way to sacrifice your future. But hey, everyone has to spend money on something. We need it to survive. And sometimes, you can buy really cool stuff with that hard-earned cash. That's what this section is all about. I'll show you how to get the most out of your spending—and how to avoid the traps and tricks of those who want your money for themselves. Pay attention—this stuff will save you a bundle.

Chapter 19
How to Spend Money

Many people have a simple money management philosophy: "If I have it, I spend it till I don't have it." Others are so good with money it makes you sick. These are the ones who save every penny they've ever found, then buy a new Porsche on their sixteenth birthday. Assuming you didn't trade your pennies for a Porsche, here are some tips to help you spend less and get more for your money.

(NOT) SPENDING TIPS

I'm guessing that you're a pro at spending money. The trick that's harder to master is *not* spending money. Try these tips.

ASK WHY

"Why do I want to buy this thing?" It's amazing how silly some of your purchases look when you ask that question.

COUNT TO 7

Live by the "7 over 7" rule: Anytime you want to buy something that costs over $7, you have to wait seven days. This will blow a big hole in your impulse buying habits!

DON'T "SAVE MONEY" BY SPENDING IT

Walk away when someone says a deal is "too good to pass up" or that "you'll never find as good a deal as this one." You will always find a better deal; keeping your money in savings is a better deal. Don't let salespeople pressure you into making decisions "before it's too late." If you shop around, you'll usually find something as good or better—or discover you didn't need the thing after all. (More on this in the next chapter!)

HANG AROUND PEOPLE WHO SPEND LESS

If the main pastime of your group of friends is shopping, chances are you're going to spend more money than you should.

WRITE IT DOWN

Every time you spend money, write down what you bought and how much you paid. Buying something isn't as easy when you have to find your expense book and write down the transaction. Hold a contest with yourself

In 1995, Americans spent $5.6 billion on movie tickets.

to see how little money you can live on each week. Set goals, and reward yourself when you meet them.

GET SOME ADVISERS

Invite two good friends with smart money habits to be your financial advisers. Whenever you want to spend more than $20 on something, you must present the idea to them and receive their unanimous approval. If they object, you can't buy it.

PLAN AHEAD

Each morning put in your wallet only the amount of money you know you'll need for that day's essentials. Keep the extra cash at home.

GIVE YOURSELF A BONUS

There's no rule that says you *must* spend all the money in your SPEND account. Put excess cash into your savings account where its value will go up instead of down.

EMPTY YOUR POCKETS

At the end of each day, dump all your pocket change in a jar. Empty the jar every month, and deposit the coins in the bank. It seems like a small amount of money, but it adds up over a year into some real cash.

In 1997, 13% of America's public schools sold fast food on campus.

BUY OFF A BAD HABIT

If you smoke, eat the wrong foods, or drink seven Cokes a day, give it up. Figure out how much money you spend on your habit, then put that money in the bank instead.

THE BEST TRICK

It just occurred to me that you may be one of those people who go through books out of order (that's what I do). So in case you're reading this chapter first, you need to know that the best trick to spending less money is to make and keep a budget based on your priorities. When you know what's most important, it's much easier to spend your money wisely. We covered all this stuff back in chapter 3, "Bonehead-Easy Guide to Money Management." Go there now and see what you've been missing.

(And if you're one of those sneaky people who read the chapter but *didn't do what it says,* go directly to chapter 3, do not pass go, and above all, do not spend another $200.)

43% of Americans aged 12 to 15 are more likely to buy a product that's advertised as specifically for teenagers.

Chapter 20

Sales Schemes You're Not Supposed to Know

Have you ever played a board game where the other players are experts who know every trick, every little-known rule, and they wipe you off the board in minutes? Welcome to the real world! Marketers—the people who make and sell the stuff you buy every day—are experts at the *selling game;* they know every trick in the book to get you to buy their stuff and pay a bundle for it. *Until now.* I'm about to show you their secrets: *price swapping, sales tricks, emotional ploys,* and all the rest. Hey, you've got to play the game—you need some of the stuff they're selling. But why not play to *win?*

DISCOUNT!

Stores use that word a lot. They want you to think you're saving lots of money by buying your stuff from them instead of someone else. Sometimes, that's true . . . and sometimes it's not. Let's look at what "discount" means to see if you're really getting a deal.

When a store announces a "50% discount," your first question should be, "Discount from *what price*?" You see, retailers deal with all sorts of prices:

- *Regular price:* This can be *anything.* Stores can sell stuff at any price they want. It can be a "discount" off some other price, or it can actually be higher than the "retail" price. They'll charge whatever people are willing to pay.

- *Retail price:* This is the price the manufacturer recommends to retailers, often called the "manufacturer's suggested retail price," or "MSRP," or simply "SRP." In the U.S., most manufacturers are prohibited from dictating a mandatory price. If they do so, it's called *price fixing.* Instead, they *suggest* a price. No retailer has to sell stuff at that price, but they can use that number to figure discounts that look really good to consumers.

- *Wholesale price:* This is the price the manufacturer or distributor offers to retailers. It's a bit more firm than the retail price, but it still fluctuates. Retailers often bargain and negotiate and wheel and deal to get a price lower than the official wholesale price.

- *Cost:* This is the price actually paid by the retailer. It's the only firm price.

So when retailers offer a discount, you need to know what price they're discounting. Chances are, they're figuring the discount on the SRP. Or they may be discounting a price that's lower or higher than the SRP. Let's say you want to buy a really nice personal headset stereo. The store's "regular" price is $160, but they're offering a 20% discount. That puts the sales price at $128. Sounds pretty good.

Then you check another store offering a 30% discount on everything in the store. That's got to be better, right? But they're figuring their discount on the *suggested retail price* of $199. That marks down the price to $139. Bigger discount, *higher* price. Then you check a third store that's offering your stereo at wholesale—$145. Biggest discount, *highest* price.

Finally, you find a store that's not even running a sale, and they'll sell you the stereo for $125. No discount, *lowest* price.

Shopping for a Personal Stereo

	regular price	discount	price
Store A (discount!)	$160	20%	$128
Store B (bigger discount!)	$199	30%	$139
Store C (wholesale!)	$145	0%	$145
Store D (no deal)	$125	0%	$125

Now you see why discounts are a tricky thing. A store can set *any* regular price, whether that figure is higher or lower than the suggested retail price. They can even advertise "wholesale" prices. In the above example, the manufacturer's wholesale price was $145, but it sold them for $100 to that particular store because they ordered 50.

What's the solution? Figure out what price a store is discounting—*not* the percentage of the discount. Better yet, just compare the bottom prices. Who cares if you're getting a "big discount"? You just want the lowest price.

SAVE BIG!

This one really bugs me. It's a philosophical thing. After reading all those chapters on how to save money, you'll be pleased to see a lot of stores encouraging you in the same thing: SAVE BIG! SAVE MORE! But they're talking about something else.

The only way to save money is . . . well, to *save it*. That means, *Don't spend it*. When a store announces that you'll "save money," what they really mean is that you'll spend *less* of it than if you shopped somewhere else. (And as we saw with that discount trick, that claim may not even be true.)

But whether you spend $145 for something, or "save" by spending just $125, you're still *spending* it. Of course, retailers don't want you to think that way. They know that if you focus on what you're *spending,* you may have second thoughts. So they try to focus on the positive side. There's nothing wrong with that. And if you truly are going to spend money anyway, then look for ways to spend less of it.

But remember, every dollar you spend is a dollar you're *not* saving. When you see a big SAVE! sign, think of it as a reminder to make a savings deposit. That's the only way you'll *really* be doing what the sign says. Okay, I'm done venting. Let's move on.

BUY NOW!

This is an emotional trick stores use to create a sense of *urgency.* They know that the moment you walk out of the store, they lose their best chance of making a sale. You'll find a better deal elsewhere or blow your money on a pizza party or have second thoughts and stick the money in your savings account. They don't want you and your money to walk away, so they use all sorts of ploys to prevent it.

They'll tell you that "time is limited"—if you come back later, the sale will be over and you'll have to pay full price. But chances are, that's not quite true. Many stores will honor the sale price even after the sale is over.

They'll tell you that "quantity is limited"—if you walk away, the item may sell out. True enough, but for all you know, they have a truckload of the stuff parked out back or can order more from the manufacturer or another store. And even if they run out, is that such a shame? Do you *really* want this stuff? If you didn't get it, would it be a big problem in your life? Walking away to think about it can be the best way to answer those questions.

They'll tell you that the "price can't be beat"—so why even bother to shop around? Maybe they do have the lowest price. But you won't know that until you shop around. When someone tells you that a deal is "too good to be true," or "a chance of a lifetime," or "you can't afford to walk away," just smile and walk away. These expressions apply to things like faith, family, friendships—seldom do they accurately describe the act of *buying stuff*. I've been buying stuff for a few decades, and I've yet to find something that could be bought with money that was worthy of these terms.

If you walk away from "buy now" ploys, you will occasionally miss out on a good deal. But the law of averages is in your favor. You'll save far more money by resisting urgent buying decisions than you ever will by succumbing to them. The rare great deal will be offset by the countless bogus or unnecessary deals you turn down.

MORE SALES TRICKS

Discounts, savings appeals, and urgency ploys are the most popular sales tricks. But there are many others. Here are a few to watch for:

BAIT AND SWITCH

The "bait" is usually an advertisement offering something at a ridiculously low price. When you go to the

In 1997, Channel One broadcast its commercially sponsored news show into 12,000 American schools.

store to check it out, the salesman tells you it was already sold, then offers you something else—*at a higher price*. For example, a dealer might advertise a killer deal on a new car. When you show up, the car has been sold, but you can buy the same model, with more features, for just $1000 more than the advertised model. You're sold.

If the ad was bogus, the trick is illegal. But the dealer doesn't have to commit fraud to use it. If you had read the ad's fine print, you would have seen that the price was for a particular vehicle, whose ID number is printed in the tiny type. *Someone* will get there first and buy the car, which is stripped down to the barest of features. The dealer sells that car at cost or even loses a few dollars on it. He can afford it, because the ad brings in many more customers who get talked into buying the same model with more features at a higher price.

If you feel like you've been taken in by a bait-and-switch trick, ask the salesperson. How many items did they have at that price? When were they sold? If things look suspicious, hold onto a copy of the ad and call the city or county office or your state's office of consumer affairs. If the store has been using this trick illegally, people are being ripped off, and that's not right. If the office receives enough complaints, they'll investigate.

UP-SELLING

This trick is used all the time. After you've placed your fast-food order, the clerk asks, "Would you like fries with your meal?" You're already spending money, so you figure, sure, a little more money won't hurt. When you buy a TV, the salesperson asks if you want the "extended warranty"—for more money, of course. And one of these days you'll rent a car, and the rental agent will try to talk you into a bigger model, insurance, more insurance, and a cellular phone. In each case, you're watching up-selling in action.

There's nothing wrong with it. If you were selling stuff, you'd want to ask people if they want more. When it's done graciously, up-selling is harmless. But when a salesperson starts piling on the pressure, it's obnoxious. And if you give into it, you spend more money, and the salesperson is rewarded for being a jerk.

Here's how to avoid giving in to this trick. First, know exactly what you want before you agree to buy it. If it's a big item like electronic gear, a computer, or something else with lots of options, write down a list of what you want. If someone pressures you to get more than you came for, refer to your list and say no. If the salesperson gets obnoxious about it, tell him. Or ask to speak to the manager. The best way to shut up high-pressure salespeople is to walk away.

PACKAGE DEALS

Stores often package more than one item together, then tell you that you're getting a lower price than if you bought each item separately. But if you don't want everything in the package, why spend more money for it? If they're offering a great deal on something if you buy a case of them, do you really need that many? It doesn't

Nearly half of American teenagers help with family grocery shopping each week.

matter if they're cheaper by the dozen if you only need one or two. Know what you came for, and leave with it.

IMPULSE BUYS

Stand at just about any checkout counter and you'll be surrounded by this trick: candy, key chains, toys, magazines, doodads—racks and stacks of cheap stuff just waiting to jump into your shopping bag. Stores put this junk at the sales counter because that's where you're most likely to make impulse buying decisions—choices without a lot of thought to them.

You're hungry, so you throw in an extra candy bar. You're bored, so you pick up that news tabloid with the inticing headline, "Elvis Spotted on Mars." And the breath mints—better snag those to combat the cheese doodles you just grabbed. You're already spending money anyway, so a few more cents isn't going to make much difference. It's kind of like up-selling, but in this case, you're the one pouring on the pressure.

Impulse buys don't just happen at the checkout counter. Anytime you make a last-minute, unplanned purchase, you're buying impulsively. If you actually like to shop, you spend lots of time in stores and are therefore more susceptible. If you're like me and dread that particular pastime, impulse buys are less of a problem. Out of sight, out of mind. The best way to avoid impulse buying is to stay out of stores. That's tough these days. The next best way is to make shopping lists and buy only those things on the list. That forces you to spend more time thinking about what you really need, and it shortens the time spent in that world of temptations. If you spot something you'd like, put it on the list and get it next time. Chances are, you won't want it then, and you can just cross it off. If you still want it, then it's not an impulse buy. It's a well-considered decision.

PLAYING THE GAME

Buying and selling is a game, and the sellers are experts at it. Salespeople practice this game every day, with dozens or hundreds of buyers. They know what will get you into their store, what will get you to buy, and how to get you to buy more than you came for. They *sell* more times each day than you *buy* in a month. That makes for a lopsided game.

Of course, it doesn't mean you shouldn't play this game. In our world, you pretty much have to. You need some of the stuff they're selling. They may be experts, but you can be a formidable amateur opponent. Use your own set of tricks:

- *Compare REAL prices.* "Discount" doesn't always mean you're getting the lowest price.

- *Save by SAVING, not by buying.* Spending is spending, which is always more expensive than money in the bank.

185

- *Buy on YOUR time, not theirs.* Saving money is an urgent need—spending works best after procrastination.

- *Leave with what YOU came for.* Don't let "bait and switch," up-selling, package deals, and impulse buys entice you into buying more than you planned.

Now you know the sales tricks and your own buying tricks. Use what you know to win the game. Just don't tell anyone where you learned these secrets.

Chapter 21

How to Buy a
Good Car

For many people, buying a car is their first big-time invest-ment. But for most of these investors, it's also their first leap into debt's bottomless pit. Can you actually buy a *good* car without going into debt? How can you keep from losing your shirt to an unscrupulous seller? I'll show you how to pay *cash* for a great, reliable, used car—and why doing it any other way is just plain silly.

THE NEW CAR MYTH

When most people dream of owning a car, they think of a *new* car. They're shiny, they're reliable, they're great fun to show off to your friends. And best of all, they have that intoxicating new-car smell.

But let's look at these benefits, compare them to what you can get with a used car, and see what they're really worth. First, there's *shiny.* Well, *any* car is shiny if it's clean and buffed and waxed—unless, of course, it's a rust bucket, and then there's not much you can do except clean up the rust. Shine is only skin deep. A good buffing job removes the oxidized paint and exposes the shiny stuff below it. Most cars can return to their new car shine for years before you have to repaint them. So this *shiny* thing is not an issue.

Let's talk about *reliable.* Yes, most new cars are more reliable than their used counterparts. And new technologies and higher quality manufacturing have been improving the reliability of cars in recent years. That also means that used cars are more reliable than ever—they're running longer and giving their owners fewer problems. What's more, some used cars are more reliable than new cars. It depends on the make and model. So while reliability is an issue, it's not an all-or-nothing thing. Let's talk more about it in a bit.

Then there's the *show-off factor.* Okay, new cars win in this class most of the time. It is more prestigious to drive into the school parking lot with the new-car sticker still in the window. But three months later, the sticker is faded, your car is dirty, and the dealer has recalled it to fix a problem you didn't even know it had. When you consider the alternative (we'll be there in a moment), prestige comes at a ridiculously high price. (And if you buy a quirky or classic used car, you may get to have your cake and eat it too.)

Finally, there's that unmistakable *new-car smell.* You can't duplicate it. You can't even retain it—the smell

fades quickly, especially if you forget and leave your gym clothes beneath the seat. In six months or less, your new car will smell like a used car. Save yourself a few thousand dollars and buy a 99¢ air freshener.

The biggest problem with a new car is the price. It's *insane.* How can people afford it? Most people can't. So they ask their bank to buy the car for them. The bank gives the car dealer most of the money, and you chip in the rest. Then you make payments to the bank. Forever. Actually, you're in debt for just 3 to 5 years, but right now in your life, that will seem like forever. You'll be halfway through college or already graduated before you actually own your whole car. For the first year, your ownership amounts to the seats, the stereo, the mirrors, and maybe the windshield wipers. You're rich.

What's worse, your car is depreciating the whole time you're pouring money into it. The car payments are based on the *new* price, not what it's worth at the moment. Depending on factors such as the interest rate, your down payment, and the market value of the car, you'll spend the first few years owing more money than the car is worth. Two years from now, you're driving a used car and paying for it like it's still new. Why not start with a used car to begin with?

This debt thing is a BIG issue. Don't even get me started on it right now, because there's no stopping me. I'll save my spiel for another chapter.

One more thing about new cars before we move on. A new car can depreciate 20% or more the *moment* you

In 1997, Americans owed $399 billion on their car loans.

drive it off the lot! Let's say you buy a new car for $15,000 (which is a cheap car these days), and change your mind a few weeks later. The dealer might give you $13,000 for it. It's hardly used! You haven't even put your gym clothes in it. Doesn't matter. It's a *used* car. You lose two grand.

You've got to ask yourself, given the high price, instant depreciation, and possibly long-term debt, *Is that new-car smell really worth it?* For most people, especially teenagers, the answer is *no.*

THE ALTERNATIVE

Good news! There's another way to go—an alternative that won't wipe out your finances now or drop you in debt's bottomless pit in the future. Here it is: *Pay cash for a good used car.*

I know that most adults think I'm crazy when I tell you this. New car dealers will boycott this book. Banks will call me a heretic. And maybe even your parents will write me nasty letters. I don't care. I'm standing my ground. Paying cash for a good used car is the only way to go.*

I've got to warn you—if you decide to follow my advice, you may be in for some serious resistance. People will tell you that buying a used car is just buying

---

* Okay, Okay, I'll qualify this statement: If you're filthy rich or your dad owns a car dealership or your last name is Ford or Toyota, *then* you can buy a new car. Leave the used cars for the rest of us.

someone else's problems. After all, why would they be selling the car if there weren't something wrong with it? Good question. Here are some good answers (and if you paid attention earlier, you already know them):

- They bought it with a loan, and now they can't afford the payments.

- They miss the prestige and new-car smell and are willing to pay for it again.

- Their needs have changed—they need a bigger car, a minivan to haul around their new baby, or a truck for their work.

- They're bored or unhappy and think that a new car will cheer them up.

- They believed someone who said that used cars are too unreliable, so they're willing to pay thousands more to eliminate that fear.

- There's something wrong with the car.

That last answer is more common with older cars. If the car is just a few years old and doesn't have a lot of miles on it, they're probably selling it for one of the other reasons. It's wise to have a mechanic check the car before you buy it. We'll come back to that idea.

Here's the *worst* excuse I've heard for going into debt to buy a new car rather than pay cash for a used one: *"Making payments teaches responsibility."* Who ever came up with this stupid idea? It uses the same logic as the

Safe Sex myth: "Debt is perfectly OK, as long as you use a *cosigner.*" Let's be real here: Debt is *not* OK. It's a stupid and painful way to buy things that go down in value. Save sex for marriage. Save debt for things that go up—like a home, a good education.

Sure, making monthly payments teaches you responsibility. So does getting pregnant and raising a baby while you're still in high school, but you don't hear adults saying that having sex and dealing with the consequences is a good way to learn responsibility. There are better ways to practice responsibility. How about making it to marriage without having sex? Or staying off drugs and alcohol? Or keeping a good job *and* doing well in school? Or putting 30% of your income into savings every paycheck? Or sponsoring a needy child in another country through regular support checks? You are *surrounded* by great ways to learn, practice, and prove your responsibility. Why on earth would you need to go into debt for this lesson?

There I go again. I said I was done talking about that debt thing till we get to that chapter. Then I jump all over this "safe debt" business. Sorry. I'm calm now. Let's continue.

BUYING A GOOD USED CAR

It's not that tough. Really. But you've got to do some homework. First, narrow down your car choices to a few makes and models. Talk to friends and relatives to find

out what they like and don't like about their cars. Then go to the library and look up these cars in the various consumer guides. The librarian will show you where to look. Some of these guides contain owners' evaluations of the vehicles—what's worked well, what's needed repair, what they like, what they don't like.

While you're at it, look for used-car price guides. These books list average prices paid for used cars by make, model, and year. In a few minutes, you'll gather volumes of information collected from hundreds of owners of each of these cars, and you'll have a rough idea of what you should expect to pay.

Now trim your list to one or two models. Pick the most reliable models from among your first list. And of course, select only those in your price range. When you've got your ideal make, model, and year chosen, you can begin reading the car ads to get an idea on prices. If you choose a rare model and year—in other words, there are few on the market—you may need to look for a long time before you find enough vehicles for sale to get an idea of what's available. You may want to broaden your preferences a bit to include other makes and models.

Here's where lots of people mess up. They spot a car in their preferred model and rush out to look at it. They fall in love (with the car, of course). It's one thing to read all the facts and figures. But as soon as they get behind the wheel, they start picturing the car as *their* car. The seller sees them drooling, so he pours on the urgency ploy; "Someone else is very interested, so if you want the car, you'd better hurry." So they make the deal, which they figure is better than letting someone else drive away in "their" car. Don't shop this way.

Instead, keep reading ads, making calls, and when you think you've found a decent vehicle, go out and see it. But don't buy it. Just look. Then go back to the ads and the phone, track down another promising vehicle, and check it out. Make sure you look at 5 to 10 cars before you buy anything. Sure, you'll pass up some deals. But you won't know if they're deals or not until you have plenty of cars to compare them to.

MAKING THE DEAL

When you finally find a car that looks good, runs well, and seems like a fair deal, go back with a parent or friend—someone who's more objective than you are. It's easy to get infatuated with a car and miss some of the troubling details. Be sure to ask the owner about the car's history of accidents and repairs. You may not get a straight answer, but it's always wise to ask. Also, ask for records of maintenance and repairs. A person who keeps a file of receipts is generally someone who takes care of cars.

If it still looks like a good deal, take it to a mechanic. He can run simple tests on the car, inspect the brakes and fluids, and tell you if there's anything scary lurking out of view. If the car has big problems, look for another—you don't want to be buying someone else's

problems. If the car passes your mechanic's inspection, make an offer.

There's an art to making a deal, and I can't possibly teach this art to you in a few paragraphs. But I can give you some tips.

First of all, buying a car is one of the few transactions that can still be negotiated. Most things in this world have printed price tags, but car prices can be haggled. Most sellers count on this fact, so they price the car higher, knowing that they'll probably be offered less. If you've done your homework, you already know the prices of similar cars, so you can make an offer that's closer to reality. But remember that the ads you read were placed by people expecting to haggle, so most or all of the *offering* prices are higher than the true *sales* price.

When you make your offer, expect the seller to counter it with a price somewhere between your two prices. After that, you're on your own. Some people will haggle and haggle. Others won't play that game. If the car has been advertised for a while, the seller may be holding out for too high a price. Leave your name and number and ask him to call you if he doesn't get a better offer. Sometimes walking away will be enough to convince him that it's time to take your offer.

Here's another important tip. Don't carry around lots of money. Believe it or not, some "sellers" advertise a low-priced car, then tell callers that lots of people have called on the ad, and "you'd better bring cash if you want to buy it." So you take $2,000 out of the bank, show up to buy

In 1995, Americans spent nearly $85 billion on new cars.

the car, and someone robs you. It could be the "seller" or someone working with the seller or just someone else who read the ad and figured that potential buyers would be showing up with great stacks of cash in hand.

So don't carry cash when you're car shopping. Bring a checkbook. If the seller insists on cash, go to your bank and ask for a cashier's check. I'll say it again: *Don't carry cash.*

One more thing before you drive away with your "new" car: Give the seller another opportunity to "fess up" about the car. Ask, "Now that I *own* this car, is there anything you can tell me to look out for in its future?" Now that the deal is done, the seller may be more forthcoming about possible problems, such as a battery that might need replacing soon, or a funny little squeak that shows up only on cold mornings, if you happen to be driving 90 MPH, and jerk the wheel to the right. All cars have their quirks, and you might as well find out about them before they get expensive.

Last tip: Many people prefer to buy their used car from a used car dealer. They figure that the car's in better shape and the seller is more honest. Not necessarily. Most used car dealers buy their cars in trades and auctions. They know very little about the car and may not have repair records or any other information on the car's history (or worse, they conveniently "lost" records that betrayed a car's troubled past). What's more, they've got to sell lots of cars each week to stay in business, so they don't spend a lot of time fixing problems in the cars they

get. Typically, they give a car a good cleaning and maybe fix some minor, obvious problems. They may even cover up nastier problems that will cost you big bucks if you buy the car.

Private sellers can be just as sneaky, but at least you'll get a better idea of the car's history. You'll also learn a lot about the car just by meeting the owner. It sounds cruel to say this, but a person who lives in a beat-up house, has another beat-up car in the driveway, and looks kind of beat-up himself is not the person you want to be buying your car from. Like dogs, cars take on the personality of their owners. When you buy from a private seller, you get a telling glimpse at the environment your car grew up in.

And to top it all off, a private party is likely to sell a car at hundreds or even thousands less than a dealer. The dealer has to make a profit. The person selling his own car is just trying to get cash to pay for another car.

Here's the best part: If you do your homework and look at lots of cars before making your choice, you'll wind up with a better deal, a more reliable car, and money left over to put back in the bank. No matter how great your car, it's not going to last forever. Start saving now to cover the maintenance and repairs required for any car. What you don't spend can go toward your *next* car. Then celebrate your success. You are among the few, the proud, the really, really smart, who know the freedom of driving their *own* car instead of one owned by the bank.

A Personal Test Drive

After writing this chapter, I put it to the test: I bought a truck. I confess I had some expert help from my friend Mike, who had also helped me write this chapter. He has made a hobby out of buying, fixing up, and selling cars. We bought our first cars together back in the 70s, and Mike has kept up the habit with several purchases each year since. Here's what happened on this latest hunt:

First, we researched makes, models, years, and prices in the buyer's guides. I picked a '91 Isuzu Trooper as my first choice. Then we spent a month reading the ads and calling the owners to get a better idea of what was available, in what condition, and for what price. We took a few of these Troopers for test drives. Finally, I found one I really liked—clean, in good condition, and raised in a good home.

The asking price was $6,900. We waited a week, and the price fell to $5,900. We took it to a mechanic for an inspection; he gave us a list of little things that were wrong with it—nothing major, but enough to give us some bargaining chips. We offered $4,500, and settled at $4,800. Cash. (I know, I broke the "don't carry cash" rule, but I had a bodyguard.)

It's a great truck! Yes, I'll have to put some money into it to fix the little things, and if I keep it too long, I'll have to fix some big things. But for the next two or three years, it will treat me as well as I treat it. And it cost me $22,000 less than a new model.

Chapter 22

How to Borrow
Money (But Don't)

The best advice for borrowing money is: *Don't.*

For many people, borrowing has become a way of life; the temptation is fierce. Paying with cash, you could barely afford a $150 stereo; by making monthly payments of just $30 you can own an $800 system. And instead of slaving away your summer earning money for a new wardrobe this fall, you can charge the clothing on a credit card and pay off the balance over several months.

It seems magical. You can own things you could never afford to buy with cash. But the truth is, you don't own them.

When you buy something on installment (make monthly payments), you don't really own it—the lender does. And they make a killing by letting you use it. Many stores and credit card companies charge you 20% (or more) annual interest on the money you owe them—that's up to 10 times the amount your bank is probably paying you for the use of your money. So while your $500 savings account earns about $25 in interest in one year, the $500 you owed during that year cost you $100 in interest.

In essence, anyone with unpaid credit card balances is lending her savings account to the bank so it can loan her her own money and charge her for the privilege (think about that one). As I mentioned earlier, borrowing money to pay for things that depreciate is like trying to go up a down escalator.

And let's stop this stupid myth: THERE'S NO SUCH THING AS "SAFE DEBT!" If you need to learn responsibility, do something positive. Don't mortgage your future to pay for today.

Now that I've made myself clear, I'll admit that certain loans, in certain circumstances, may be acceptable. Let's look at various kinds of loans, how they work, and how to save yourself from the trouble they can cause.

Borrowing Money from Family and Friends

If you borrow any amount of money, whether it's $5 or $5,000, give the lender an IOU note showing how much you borrowed, when you borrowed it, the amount of the interest, if any, and when he can expect to be paid back. Write out a copy for yourself and put the payback date on your calendar. If you can't pay back on the date you

promised, tell the person *beforehand*—don't put him in the uncomfortable position of having to ask you for his own money.

INSTALLMENT LOANS

An installment loan is one that you pay off in a series of payments rather than all at once. It's also called an *amortized* loan. Figuring out the interest on an installment loan is a bit confusing.

With a *normal* loan of $100 at 15% interest for one year, you return the $100 and pay $15 in simple interest at the end of the year.

But with an *installment* loan, you'd pay only $8.31 in interest. That's because you only had their $100 for the first month. Each month you gave a little bit back, and you only paid interest each month on the amount you owed for that month.

In other words, a 12-month installment loan is really like *12 loans.* Let's say you buy a $500 TV with $50 of your own money and finance the rest with the appliance store at 18% annual interest. What you've really done is borrowed $450 from a finance company that works with the store. They bought your TV for you by giving the store $450 in cash. Now they want you to pay them back.

The first month's loan is for $450 at 1.5% ($\frac{1}{12}$ of 18%). You owe them $6.75 in interest. If you send them a check for $456.75, you'll be completely paid up. Unfortunately, you don't have that much.

All you can afford is $41.25, so you send them that much. The finance company uses $6.75 to pay your interest and applies the rest—$34.50—to pay down your $450 debt. Now you owe them $415.50 ($450 minus $34.50), which they're willing to loan to you for the next month at 1.5% interest.

At the end of the month you owe them $6.23 in interest ($415.50 x 1.5%). You send them another check for $41.25—$6.23 for the interest, $35.02 to help pay off the debt. Now you owe $380.48, which they loan to you for another month at 1.5% interest.

As long as you don't pay off the loan, they just extend it for another month at 1.5% interest. If you continue to pay them $41.25 a month, it will take you 12 months to pay it off.

The rule with installment loans is that the larger your payment and the quicker you pay off the loan, the less interest you pay. Let me show you. Here's a $5,000 car loan at 12% annual interest:

paid off in . . .	monthly payment	total you pay
1 year	$444	$5,331
2 years	$235	$5,650
5 years	$111	$6,678

Here's a $100,000 home loan at 10% annual interest:

paid off in . . .	monthly payment	total you pay
1 year	$8,792	$105,499
10 years	$1,322	$158,582
30 years	$ 878	$316,063

As you can see, long-term loans cost a bundle in interest! In that house example, you'll pay 3 times the amount of the original loan by the time you're done paying it off. But even smaller and shorter loans take a chunk out of your finances.

LOAN AGREEMENTS

If you're under 18, lenders won't let you borrow their money unless you have an adult cosigner. Whether you have a cosigner or not, never sign a loan agreement until you've taken it home to study the terms carefully. The agreement, or "note," will list the *principal* (the amount of money you're borrowing), *finance charge* (the interest), *other charges* (late payment fee, early repayment penalty, etc.), *payment information* (the amount, the due dates, where to send them), and *total of payments* (how much you will really pay them by the time the loan is through).

If you end up getting a loan, make the payments on time. If your payment is late, the lender will usually report this to a credit bureau; everyone looking at your credit report will know. If you mess up two or three times in one year, it looks really bad.

If the loan has no early repayment penalty (can you believe you'd get in trouble for paying back someone too *soon*?), pay it off as rapidly as possible. Even with an extra $10 in each payment, you'll pay it off much faster and save interest. If you have money in a bank account and you don't need it for a couple of years, use it to pay off the loan. Then deposit your monthly loan payment into your bank account instead. You'll be the one earning interest on the payments instead of the lender.

INVESTMENT BORROWING

The only time buying on credit is a smart investment is when the thing you buy will *increase* in value. If the amount of its appreciation (increase) is greater than the cost of the loan, then it may be worth borrowing for. Here are some instances where borrowing may be wise:

BUSINESS INVESTMENT

Let's say you're really good at desktop publishing. You know you could produce flyers, brochures, and newsletters for several clients if you could buy a computer and software. If your business plan shows that you could afford the interest on a loan and still make a healthy profit, then borrowing money may be a smart business investment. Depending on your tax situation, the interest on such a loan may be deductible as a business expense.

EDUCATION

A good education is an investment in your future. If you need to borrow money to get one, then the interest on the loan is a part of the investment. Student loans allow you to postpone repayment until you're out of school and in a job. At the same time, a loan is a loan; if you run up a big bill, you'll be paying for it long after you've forgotten how much fun those all-night study sessions were.

REAL ESTATE

The right piece of property in the right location for the right price will go up in value even after interest and inflation. Real estate investments generally require a hefty down payment, a steady monthly income, and several years to appreciate significantly—all factors that make it difficult for teenagers to invest.

I know my no-borrowing advice is a lonely call in this world where debt is the American way to buy things. But just because most people borrow money, it doesn't make it right. With very few exceptions, borrowing money is just plain stupid. If you can't figure out a way to buy something without going into debt, you're not thinking hard enough. Or you want something that's too expensive.

Your budget and money-management tools are your best hope of avoiding this awful trap. Don't borrow against your future to pay for what you need *today*. Instead, start *saving* today to pay for your future. I promise you, when your future arrives, it will thank you for it.

Chapter 23

Setting an All-Time Credit Record

Your credit record is your financial reputation. If you want to rent an apartment, buy a house, get a phone hooked up, get a credit card, take out a loan, buy a blimp, or start a business, you need a good record.

A company that wants to check your credit can call other companies that have done money deals with you in the past, or they can get a report from a credit reporting bureau. But if you've never been granted credit in the past, you don't *have* a credit record. Where do you start?

Fortunately, you don't always need a credit record. Some credit grantors realize that no record is better than a bad one. If you don't have one, they'll look more carefully at other information on your credit application:

- *Income.* The longer you've held a job, the better you'll look. Don't lie about your salary or how long you've worked there; they may call your boss to verify the numbers. If you have other sources of income—side jobs, allowance, whatever—be sure to list these too. Every little bit helps. Save your check stubs. If someone pays you in cash, make out a bill, mark it "paid," and have her sign it. Make sure that the money you earn can be used to prove your ability to earn more of it.

- *Expenses.* You may be asked to list some of your regular expenses such as rent and car insurance. If they don't ask, don't volunteer it; and if they do, list only what is asked for.

- *Assets.* List the amount of money you have in savings and checking accounts (they'll call to verify these, too, so shoot straight). If you have money invested in mutual funds, CDs, stocks, bonds, gold, or pork belly futures, write it down. Be ready to provide the name of the firm that handles these investments for you. These things suggest that you know how to handle your money. You may wish to mention any toys or vehicles you own that are worth several hundred dollars or more: an expensive camera, motorcycle, car, or Bell Jet Ranger helicopter.

- *Liabilities.* If you have any debts—auto or personal loans, charge cards—you'll be asked to list your monthly payment and the outstanding balance.

If your monthly expenses all but wipe out your income, they'll figure you don't have enough cushion to make monthly payments on a loan or credit card debt. If your liabilities (what you *owe*) greatly exceed your assets (what you *own*), they don't want to help you dig your grave deeper. (Actually they know that once you're *in* the grave, you won't leave enough behind to pay off the debt.)

But if you have a healthy cash flow, low or no debt, and evidence of good money management habits, you're their kind of customer.

STEPS TO BUILD CREDIT

1. If you're 18 or older, apply for a credit card from Sears, Montgomery Ward, or another large department store. These are typically the easiest to qualify for.

2. When you get the card, use it to make one small purchase each month for six months. Make sure it's something you would have bought that month anyway, or charge something your parents need and have them reimburse you for it.

3. **Pay your balance in full the moment you get the bill!** If you bounce a check or make a late payment, you'll defeat your purpose. By paying the balance in full you avoid paying

interest on the "loan," which would waste your money.

4. Each month your payment record is sent to the credit bureau. They will begin a credit record on you, which will be spotless due to your outstanding payment habits.

5. Apply for your next charge card. If your application is accepted, you may wish to close your first card's account by cutting the card in half.

The U.S. stopped making dimes and quarters out of silver in 1965.

Chapter 24

A Short List of
Things You Can't Buy

I knew a man whose monthly house payment was $30,000. Working 22 weekdays a month, he had to earn $1,364 per day: that's $136 *every hour* of a ten-hour day. Of course he had to earn over twice that much to pay for his family's cars, boats, vacations, clothes, insurance, food, and orthodontist bills.

I knew a woman who spent at least $20,000 every month on clothes and jewelry alone. It was worse around Christmas.

I knew a man in Haiti who earned about $300 per year to support his family of six. They lived in a mud and reed hut: dirt floor, no water, no heat, no electricity.

All of these people had something in common; they couldn't afford what they wanted.

The first man struggles to make his house payment—some months he falls behind. I know what you're thinking; why doesn't he sell his $3 million home and settle for something he can afford . . . like a *$2 million* home? But in *his* world, that would be an embarrassing step backwards. Kind of like if you and your friends all drove beautiful new cars, but you had to sell yours and buy a clunky used one.

The woman struggles to pay her credit card bills every month, but she carries a $10,000 unpaid balance. There never seems to be enough money in her checking account to pay it off completely, so she pays an extra $150 in finance charges each month. Sure, she could try to limit her fashion purchases to just $15,000 a month, but there's always some new occasion that demands another $5,000 dress: a party, dinner in Rome, a night at the ballet. (Would *you* wear the same dress to every formal occasion?)

And my friend in Haiti would like a wood house, better education for his sons, and a mule; but he always runs out of money before he runs out of needs.

It's a fact: You will *never* be able to afford what you want. The reason has something to do with *materialism.* Materialism is the tendency to put more value on physical things than on spiritual or intellectual things. Like when you eat, get high, have sex, make money, or buy things just to bring you happiness.

The problem with materialism is that the happiness it delivers is never *quite* enough to fill the need you have. So you keep buying, eating, drinking, sleeping around, or whatever, but you never feel satisfied.

One of the most popular forms of materialism is *consumerism,* whose followers play by the rule, "Whoever dies with the most toys wins." To play, you keep buying

"Whoever loves money never has money enough; whoever loves wealth is never satisfied with his income." —Solomon

toys and clothes, stereos and CDs, shoes and electronic gadgets, cars and anything else you think will give you pleasure . . . until you run out of money or die.

Unfortunately, the companies that sell these things tell you that their products will bring you the very things you feel you're missing on the inside—jeans that make every guy stop and pay attention, a car that identifies you as the cool person you want to be, shoes that let you fit in with the right crowd, high-performance toys that announce to the world that you know how to have fun. But if you've played this game at all, you know that the promises of the advertisers are mostly empty. You *know* the feeling. You've felt the thrill of buying some really great stuff with your own money, only to have that thrill shrink to a sense of profound emptiness when the stuff doesn't satisfy the void you feel inside. It's more than buyer's remorse, it's a deep longing for something you can't buy.

If the material world cannot fill the need you have in your heart, then there are two possibilities: Either life is a cruel joke—a frustrating and pointless search for a satisfaction you can never have—or it's time to discover that there's a spiritual side to you which, having been created by God, will never be satisfied until you're connected with him.

I'm certain it's the latter.

So make money. Give some of it away. Save up a stack of it. And spend what's left. But while you're making all these transactions, remember this: *It's only money.*

Barcode: 31833033165769
Title: Money : how to make it, spend ...
Type: BOOK
Due date: 4/15/2011,23:59

Barcode: 31833056323832
Title: How to make someone fall in lo...
Type: BOOK
Due date: 4/15/2011,23:59

Barcode: 31833043128419
Title: The encyclopedia of drugs and ...
Type: BOOK
Due date: 4/15/2011,23:59

Barcode: 31833059630324
Title: Dream walker : a memoir : a jo...
Type: BOOK
Due date: 4/15/2011,23:59

Total items checked out: 4

Telephone Renewal: 421-1240
Website Renewal: www.acpl.info

A Short List of *Money* Things You Can't Buy

It won't buy you *joy,* it can't fill your life with *purpose.* It will never satisfy your need for *love.* These items are too expensive. Their price is so outrageous that there's just one Person in the entire universe rich enough to buy them—and he already owns them (he invented them).

The strange thing is, *he bought them anyway.* Not for himself, but for *us.* God *bought* us joy, purpose and love, paying for these gifts with the life of his own son Jesus. When we try to satisfy our own spiritual hunger through *stuff,* it's like a slap in God's face: "Thanks for the great gifts, but if you don't mind, I'd kinda like to shop for something else!"

Stop looking. What you *really* need, you cannot buy. God bought it for you, with the most precious treasure he had. Just accept his priceless gifts. And then say thanks by giving him *your* treasures—your money, your job, your relationships, your future, *yourself.* It's the best investment you'll ever make, paying interest daily . . . and dividends forever.

More great tips
F O R   T E E N S

Life Happens
Get Ready (For Teens) and *Help Your Teenager Get Ready for It* (For Parents)
BARRY ST. CLAIR

One idea, two points of view! Both books in the *Life Happens* series address how young people can discover their place in the world. One book talks to teens about how they can find their calling in God's world. The second tells parents how they can help their teenagers move ahead with confidence in making decisions about careers, marriages, and the future.

Teen Book - 0-8054-6294-5 • Adult Book - 0-8054-6295-3

What Would Jesus Do?
GARRETT W. SHELDON
WITH DEBORAH MORRIS

A contemporary re-telling of one of the most popular Christian books ever — *now in paperback.*

Thirty million people were inspired by the vibrant message of Charles M. Sheldon's *In His Steps*. A century later, Garrett W. Sheldon follows in the steps of his great-grandfather with a contemporary version of the same timeless story. *What Would Jesus Do?* captures all the energy and depth of its predecessor but is told in the context of today's society, making the story more applicable and accessible to modern readers. Entertaining and challenging, this gripping narrative of a congregation's collective commitment to walk in the footsteps of Jesus encourages all Christians to dedicate their lives completely.   0-8054-0189-X

Available at fine bookstores everywhere